The Color of Time

Dear Karen.

thanks so very

much for the

chance to

share

my thoughts

with the students

of SND,

Clive Matson

The Color of Time

How my wife and I dealt with five generations of changing attitudes toward our inter-racial marriage.

My life on the edge of change

More of my howling into the winds of injustice and being surprised when someone listened.

ABE — MARKMAN

Cover Page photo by Jefferson Siegal, *The Villager vol. 79, no. 29 (2009, December 23--29)*

Photo of Mayor Bill de Blasio and Family by Kathy Willens, *AP and Gotham Gazette, September 11, 2013*

ISBN-13: 9780692987308
ISBN-10: 0692987304

Dedicated to Charlotte and Chandy
They left us too soon

About the Author

A be Markman had a sixty-year career as youth center director and co-founder and CEO of a highly successful social service nonprofit, The Neighborhood Self-Help by Older People Project.

Two of his essays were published by *The Humanist* magazine, "First Person: Overcoming Hidden Biases" and "Why Are So Many Black Americans Killed by the Police?"

In recognition of his activism and courage in pursuit of justice, he was awarded the 2010 Community Service Award by The New York Society for Ethical Culture — his spiritual home.

Contents

Section 1

A small group of people can change the world,
It's the only thing that ever has.

— Margaret Mead

Introduction

*B*y Gary Markman (Younger cousin of the author, a published writer and faculty member of the Sacred Heart University in Connecticut. Abe and Gary discovered each other in 2012, and Gary edited an early version of this book.)

The year was 1953. The Korean War had ended. Frank Sinatra signed his first contract with Capitol Records. Mickey Mantle hit the longest home run ever recorded. John F. Kennedy married Jacqueline Bouvier.

And Abe Markman committed a felony, because he married a black woman, Charlotte Cochran, the love of his life.

To be fair, the marriage was only a felony in twenty-seven of our then forty-eight freedom-loving states. And perhaps, to make up for the remaining nine, Abe's family, the Markmans, of which I am a charter member, "excommunicated" him.

The fact that Charlotte was bright, articulate, a college graduate, and an artist was irrelevant. The fact that the members of Charlotte's family were pillars of the Atlanta community — albeit the black Atlanta community, was irrelevant. The fact that Charlotte's father was an MD and a close friend of the Rev. Martin Luther King Sr., was irrelevant.

Charlotte Cochran was black. *That* was relevant.

At the time I was only eight years old and completely unaware of either Abe or the cruel and absurd laws that were channeling his life. It wasn't until another eight years had passed (and still six years before the Academy Award winning movie *Guess Who's Coming to Dinner* was released) that I even heard

Abe's name. This came via a one-liner from my father in a chance conversation that went something like this, "Boy, it's hot for April. By the way, did I ever mention that I have a cousin, Abe, who was kicked out of the family for marrying a black woman?" The only thing he left out was, "Please pass the salt."

That bothered me. A lot. And the idea of this mysterious Abe person stayed with me through the years. I knew nothing about his life, but I did know that if he married the woman he loved while standing up to his family, and also a largely prejudicial society, he was a hero. And, at that time, based on my teenage observations, we Markmans were sorely lacking heroes.

Fast forward past the explosion of the Internet. I posted a note on a family genealogy website inquiring about Abe. To my amazement, over a half-century after my father's, "By the way …" I received an e-mail from none other than Abe Markman himself.

I couldn't wait to meet him, but he informed me that, unfortunately, I would have to wait a bit longer. For the next two months, he would be busy organizing a rally in Central Park to protest global warming.

Abe was eighty-five years old at the time.

The Arc

I want to say that this story chronicles the life of an amazing man. But "amazing" is an inadequate word. From his almost unique experiences living through some of the terrible days of race relations—through their eventual evolution—Abe's experiences are both tragic and courageous. The tragedy was the loss of his daughter at age twenty-five and his wife at age sixty-seven.

He showed his courage while raising his family in Manhattan's Lower East Side. Abe took his years of experience as a social worker, and, inspired by the kinds of lives his wife and daughter led as leaders themselves, he devoted his life to working as a social activist. As a white Jewish man, his unlikely role as mediator and instructor to gangs and the New York City Police Department has not only been credited with saving lives—both of gang members and of officers—but also resulted in his being chosen Chair of The Lower East Side Call for Justice, a highly influential activist group.

His tireless efforts over a twenty-year period were instrumental in changing police policy regarding off-duty officers' carrying their weapons when they would be drinking. Abe was also fully engaged in having the Rockefeller Drug Laws changed, and in the process was arrested by police during a demonstration in what was actually a humorous incident. Abe writes about this in one of three stories about the Call for Justice.

In Part III, "The Color of Action," there are other stories. They reveal Abe's ability to engage small and large groups in solving neighborhood and societal problems.

Preface

I t has been suggested that I write two books, one based on the title, *The Color of Time*, that focuses on how I and my African American wife dealt with five generations of changing attitudes to our marriage; and one based on the subtitle,

My Life on the Edge of Change, that adds a series of essays of my howling into the wind against injustice and being surprised when someone listened.

Although I confess to limitations in connecting these and other significant aspects of my life, I believe you would barely know who I am without at least a sampling of my personal and public adventures into the unknown.

My observations were influenced by years as an inner-city social group worker and activist, and as a white man married in 1953 to a brown-skinned woman, Charlotte Elaine Cochran.

At that time, entering such a union was considered by many as an outrageous affront to their sensibilities and beyond acceptable behavior.

What mattered most to us, however, was the devotion we had to each other, to the success of our marriage, and to our children and grandchildren. They came into our arms and our world with distinct colors, hair textures, personalities, and abilities.

How we all fared and adapted was heavily dependent on whether we were born before, during, or after the civil rights movement of the 1960s. I have tried to describe as sensitively as possible both our own and other people's reactions to each of us separately and as a family.

On a November day in 1952, I began an experience that I still cannot fully grasp. It was the day I met Charlotte, who would become my wife. Within a short period of time, my sense of the world changed profoundly.

I didn't think to write this memoir, however, until my son, Michael, set a deadline four years ago. He wanted me to write the stories of my life for his children, my grandchildren and all of who followed us. I was more comfortable writing essays. So this book is somewhat like a series of essays and sketches.

As my son reminds me, this book is not just about our family; it is about me. It is mainly about my determination since childhood to prove mostly to members of my premarriage/all white family, and to myself — that I could overcome considerable limitations.

As the youngest by far both among my four siblings and my preteen peer group, I was often thought of as "the kid who couldn't keep up" and that my ambitions were well beyond my capabilities. I felt the pain of being seriously misjudged, mistreated, and underestimated by some. Yet I also felt the joy of being profoundly inspired by others.

Despite having felt humiliation in school as a very slow reader, I discovered in my twenties that I had several valuable traits and abilities. I could conceptualize the meaning of some societal phenomena and think of creative ways to resolve seemingly intractable inter-personal and public issues. I attained skills in organizing and leading small groups, pursuing and sometimes opening paths toward a niche of progressive change and social justice. As I felt mistreated, I had empathy for others in similar or much worse circumstances. Sometimes, no matter what I did resulted in failure. At other times I was able to anticipate, reach for, navigate, and inspire ethical and progressive change.

I was fortunate as a white person to witness and experience from an intimate vantage point the rich culture, courage, and resilience of many people of color. On the other hand, I also observed and sometimes felt—but could only imagine—the daily drumbeat of the unjust treatment they faced.

I divided this book into two sections. The first section describes my experiences as:

- a white man of Jewish heritage in a black world
- an inner-city community social group worker
- an activist, and
- a neophyte writer but at times a published essayist.

Charlotte and I learned before and during our marriage that we were not fully prepared for what we faced, and the world was definitely not prepared to face us. The book deals with the following topics:

In Section 2, among other aims, I tried to describe my parents more fully and how they had a profound effect both on our large Jewish clan and the ethnic soul that exists both proudly and uncomfortably inside of me. If I included these detailed sketches earlier, they probably would have been a distraction from the main themes. My hope, however, is that Section 2 helps strengthen some of the book's bonds of connective tissue.

So, please accept my invitation to the color of my time and a vision of our tomorrow.

Section 1

PART I
The Life I Chose

One

The Color of a Marriage

Anti-miscegenation laws were a part of American law since before the United States was established and remained so until ruled unconstitutional in 1967 by the U.S. Supreme Court in Loving v. Virginia.

—Wikipedia

Marrying Charlotte Cochran in 1953 defined who I was for many people for the rest of my life. I was the white man who married the little, highly regarded, widely beloved, dark-brown-skinned, human dynamo.

Since our marriage I have been comfortable thinking of myself as white, despite facing heavy doses of racism that blacks can hardly ever turn off but that I can.

Charlotte and I began witnessing the world transforming before our eyes from the day we met in September, 1952. Charlotte Elaine Cochran Markman was born July 14, 1924, in Atlanta, Georgia, to Dr. Horace Bruce Cochran and Ruth Sewell Cochran. Her father was a physician, and her mother was a librarian. She was their first child, followed in two years by her sister Helen.

I was born Abraham Markman on April 24, 1926, in Brooklyn, New York. My father, Isidore Markman, was a costume jeweler, and my mother,

Mary Goldberg Markman, was a homemaker. I was their fifth and last child, and I had two brothers and two sisters.

Contrary to the consensus attitude of that era—that whites and blacks had little in common—Charlotte and I had lots in common: we both left home in our early twenties in anger at members of our family; and as soon as we met, we realized that we were exceedingly comfortable with each other.

We both came from families with fathers whom we loved and admired, and who loved us deeply in return. Our fathers pursued different careers, but in a broad sense, they were both entrepreneurs. As mentioned, my father owned and operated a costume jewelry business. Charlotte's father was a primary care physician in private practice. Both families owned fairly large and comfortable homes. My father was self-educated and well read, whereas Charlotte's father had the formal education of an MD.

Our fathers were leaders. My father led our large, Jewish extended family. Charlotte's father was a leader in their Southwest, Atlanta community, and among his patients were prominent religious and academic friends. Among them were Martin Luther King Sr. and Benjamin Mays, president of Morehouse College and a role model and mentor to Martin Luther King Jr.

Both of our fathers were very interested in public affairs: mine in electoral politics, Charlotte's in civil rights.

We both had mothers who constantly angered us. My mother expected me to live up to her need for status, and I failed continuously. Charlotte's mother and sister were cold emotionally and dismissive of Charlotte's progressive attitudes and activism. They were obsessed with acting so that they would not be looked upon as poor, uneducated, black people. Charlotte was appalled by their arrogance toward darker-skinned blacks. I did have siblings whom I liked very much but also one who echoed my mother's constant criticism of almost everything I did.

By marrying we were formally declaring to ourselves and to those concerned the profound love we shared. Today interracial marriages are much more common. In 1953, they were rare, and in a majority of states, unlawful. It shocked and unnerved people. It was especially unusual in those days for a white man to marry a black woman. The stereotype was that only "fallen" white women married black men. I do not recall a stereotype of a white man married to a black woman, perhaps, because it hardly ever happened.

Charlotte and I not only enjoyed identifying what we had in common, but we knew how important it would be to acknowledge our differences. I grew up with fear of and prejudice against blacks, but Charlotte was accepting and relaxed with whites. She harbored biases, however, toward Hispanics and Germans. We vowed to learn to control and even rid ourselves of these unwanted attitudes.

As indicated, I had trouble keeping up in school and often felt intense shame. I tried mightily to succeed, despite being the last in my first-grade class to learn how to read. During my last years in college, I began to realize that I had other intelligences that I could build upon: emotional, political, leadership, creative thinking, and resiliency. I started to become aware of these budding strengths when I gave up trying to become a physicist and chose a path that led to a professional degree in social group work. Although physics proved much too difficult, my curiosity of how the universe came into existence remained and is still a major interest of mine.

Charlotte, on the other hand, was an honor student in high school and a straight-A student in college. In addition, she had social, leadership, and artistic skills. Although she also enrolled in a master's degree program in social group work, she completed only one year of the two-year program.

Charlotte was more to the left politically, but after discussions, she would usually agree with me. I didn't know if that was due to my persuasiveness or her belief that a woman has to find ways to massage her husband's ego.

Long before we married, Charlotte became emotionally independent of her family. It was her strength that I tried to emulate while struggling with the emotional pain of standing up to my own family.

We needed to channel the anger at being rejected by some members of each of our families. That need was met as we formed a deep, loving relationship. It was also met by our instinctual outrage at the injustices directed against us, our children, and within the wider society.

We wanted the marriage to succeed as a way to counter the fierce rejection by some of our loved ones. We wanted to show the world that we could be good for each other. At the same time, we were determined to try to make the world a little better for people who were being treated much worse than we ever were.

Two

Falling in Love

In 1953, 27 states banned interracial marriages.

—LovingDay

I don't believe I could have been so completely relaxed with Charlotte from the moment we met if I hadn't had previous experiences with persons of color. As an example, I had a date with a brown-skinned woman in 1950 during my senior year of college.

She lived in Harlem, and one Sunday afternoon, I took the bus to meet her. There were several older women coming from church, wearing large, colorful hats. If I remember correctly, their hats were orange and yellow. Those were not the colors and styles of women's hats that I had previously seen, and my prejudices and stereotypes hit me between the eyes.

I was shocked at my own reaction and at the realization that I was not in control of my own bias. Subsequently, I told the young woman I was not ready for an interracial relationship and why. She asked if I dated her just to write about it. I said, "I might write about it someday, but that is not why I wanted to get to know you." As active students taking evening classes, we kept up a dialogue on her belief in, and my skepticism of, Marxism, but on a platonic level.

Charlotte and I first met in the fall of 1952 at Irvington House, a research institution for adolescent children with rheumatic fever. The building, located in Irvington, a small town in Westchester County, New York, lay on a steep slope overlooking a magnificent view of the Hudson River. At age twenty-five, this was my second full-time job since college.

My first job was at the Wiltwyck School for Boys. It was located in another small town in upstate New York called Esopus. Wiltwyck was a camp-like residence for boys aged eight to twelve who were remanded there by the courts, often because they were deemed unmanageable by their parents. I was hired as a counselor. After one year I was fully convinced that I was not able to maintain discipline with my group, and so I resigned.

I took that job and the one at Irvington House for four reasons: I wanted to help boys in difficult circumstances, and, while I tried to gain acceptance into a two-year social work master's degree program, I wanted to obtain comparable experience, have an income, and have a place of residence after vowing in 1950 to never live under the same roof as my mother, whom I saw, at that time, as my eternal harasser.

At Irvington House I served a group of boys, aged fourteen to sixteen, as one of three counselors. I was hired last. We each took an eight-hour shift. They had radically different ways of organizing the boys' schedules and administering their medication, and they didn't even communicate with each other. When I started, the boys were very testy. I asked the other counselors if we could meet to agree on a common routine for our group. They refused and dismissed my concerns, claiming that the group "didn't give them any trouble."

I was perplexed and worried. Had that happened later in my career, I would have threatened to report their unprofessionalism to the administrators. Instead, I met with the boys alone. I told them that I was flexible and that we could try to work out an agreeable routine when I was with them. We did, and it helped somewhat, but the boys had so much pent-up anger that they were still hard to control.

It was ironic that Charlotte, who knew of the difficulties I was having with my group, would call on me to calm down her group of girls.

When Charlotte was hired at Irvington House, she was short, thin, and effervescent. In contrast, I was much taller and heavier but more sedate. She told me that when she first got the job, she spoke to another black female counselor and asked if there were any eligible men on staff. The counselor informed her that there were, but that they were all white. Charlotte said, "That's not a problem."

We first met walking to a staff-sponsored spaghetti party. Charlotte greeted me with a radiant smile of acceptance that I had never felt before from any other human being.

The senior counselors arranged for the spaghetti party so that all the counselors could become better acquainted. My most vivid memory was seeing Charlotte gliding across the room with her small body aglow with swaying, joyous movement.

Living on campus, we became fast friends. I asked Charlotte about her plans, and she told me that she was going to marry a jazz musician in Ohio. As I was beginning to have strong feelings for her, I pointed out the difficulties of being with someone who was constantly moving from gig to gig. She said that she also wondered about that. We spent a good deal of time in each other's rooms, became sexually intimate, and, after many hours of talking, listening, and questioning each other seven days a week for six months, we felt confident that the feelings we had for each other would be lasting, and we decided to get married.

Charlotte was concerned that we would not have many friends. I said that we would have each other, and if we found others who accepted us and became our friends, that would be a plus. We really didn't have to worry about making friends, because when we left Irvington House, the staff organized a fun-filled engagement party for us at the International Hotel. Some of these good people remained dear friends for life.

For the most part, wherever we lived, we were surrounded by friends. We were both human magnets in our own right before we met, and we were more so as a couple.

As we became more involved, we began discussing what we thought might become problems later unless we were open with each other. I explained to

Charlotte that I grew up in a family where most of its members thought black people were beneath their status. As a result, I became and still was very prejudiced. (Later in life I learned that my prejudice arose within me—as it does with most people—from infancy and well before direct parental influence becomes an important factor in the growth of personality.)

As mentioned, Charlotte said that she, too, was prejudiced but not against whites, but rather against Germans and Puerto Ricans. We vowed to work hard to overcome our negative attitudes. Later in our life together, I found her lack of explicit or implicit bias against whites as a race was truly authentic. Many other whites who knew Charlotte signaled in one way or another that they felt fully relaxed and accepted in her presence. That was the case, unless she thought you were arrogant or had other specific traits that bothered her.

Our fathers and other family members were apoplectic on finding out about our intention to marry. I had never seen my father so angry, but Charlotte and I never hesitated in our resolve to become husband and wife.

On our days off from Irvington House, we stayed at the well-managed International Hotel in Harlem. The female in charge was quite accepting of us, and Charlotte and I relished our moments together.

We chose that hotel so that we could be isolated from the parts of Harlem whose residents often looked at us with fury in their eyes as we passed by their corner hangouts. I still clearly remember some of the men whose facial expressions sent a message of outrage: how dare a white man parade before them with one of their black "sisters," a sister who was telling them—by the simple fact that she was with me—that they were not good enough for her. Those were scary moments that we tried to completely avoid. Charlotte, having lived at the YMCA in Harlem before we met, knew of several other places in Harlem where we would be accepted, and the International Hotel was one of them.

During our times at work, it became obvious to both the staff and the children that Charlotte and I were having an affair. When Charlotte called on me to calm down her group at bedtime, I was invariably greeted by one of the older, more attractive girls, who would shout out from a curled-up, seductive position on her cot, "Hi, Abie baby." There were other times when other children gave off knowing signals.

Except for the other two counselors assigned to my group, who showed no overt interest in us as a couple, the staff's attitude toward us ranged from enthusiastic acceptance to mild "wait and see" levels of doubt over our growing relationship. Charlotte and I learned afterward that one of our friends—who was the most supportive supervisor I ever had and someone I felt very close to—had been quite troubled about the interracial nature of our relationship, but he hid his feelings from us. Despite this, he introduced us to Phil Craft and Dave Leiman, whose acceptance of our marriage was immediate and lifelong.

Fairly often, our friends among the counselors at Irvington House would pile into a few cars, sit on each other's laps, and ride the short distance to Tarrytown for pizza or bowling parties. We had great fun, poured beer on our supervisors' heads, and insisted that Charlotte keep track of the score sheets after she failed to hit even one pin after several tries.

When Charlotte and I paired off and walked the streets of Tarrytown, we saw the clear signs of surprise and shock on the faces of the villagers. A driver of one car looked at us while we were walking along the street and was so distracted that she let her car bump into the rear of another car!

Back at work, other children were showing signs of assuming that Charlotte and I were sexually intimate. When the director learned of this, she called us into her office. She was very tactful and understanding, but she explained that our relationship was starting to "absorb the oxygen" in the institution and interfere with its ability to discover breakthrough remedies for rheumatic fever.

She also feared that our romantic relationship would be very distracting to the children. She thanked us for our service, which, with the help of our supervisors, had improved, but said that we could not continue on staff. Perhaps because we accepted the director's decision, our friends on staff did as well, and there was no backlash among the other employees upon our leaving Irvington House.

During the six months of our courtship, I observed more of Charlotte's ploys aimed at convincing me to marry her. When I voiced concern about our both being out of a job, she concocted a tall tale. She said she had spoken to the head of a settlement house in Pittsburgh that she knew and that we could both have jobs there. So off we went to Pittsburg. While on our way, Charlotte insisted that she visit the director alone. It was my naïveté not to question that.

There were no jobs, but during the trip to Pittsburgh, another side of Charlotte was revealed to me. On the 125th Street railroad station, while waiting for the train, Charlotte recognized and walked right up to acclaimed singer Marian Anderson and told her about us. Ms. Anderson was the first African American woman to sing at the Metropolitan Opera and was a civil rights hero as well.

She was also married to a white man! Ms. Anderson invited us to visit her at her home in Connecticut and wrote a note on the inside cover page of Charlotte's paperback book.

SCAN OF 64 YEARS OLD PAPER BACK BOOK PAGE

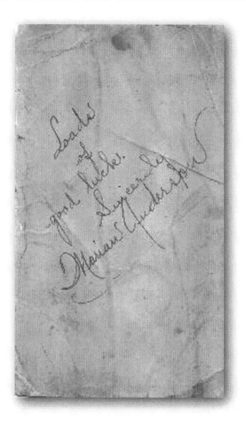

Here is the last of Charlotte's techniques to secure her hold on me: About two years before I met Charlotte, I wrote an essay about what I believed could become a new-world, secular religion. The core idea was that humans needed to unite, and the best way to do that was to work together across all borders and tribal lands as one family to find out how the universe came into being and to learn whether the universe has a purpose.

Charlotte pretended that she agreed with me and even went along as I visited groups that were willing to listen to my arguments. She did not say anything at those meetings, which should have alerted me to her real feelings. Soon after we married, I realized that she was devoted to her Christian beliefs. She practiced them much more in deeds than in pews. She attended church once a year at Christmas and often when she carried home-cooked meals for the church lunch program for the homeless.

Later in our marriage, she spoke to me of how she was taught to act like the man was in control of the family. She even told me she knew most men had "one-nighters" with women, and if I did, she didn't want to hear about it.

Charlotte really did not have to go to such lengths to convince me to marry her. Even if I didn't always see through all of it, I enjoyed most of it. I recognized what many others did all through our marriage, and that was that I was marrying one terrific person and a fighter for what is right. These shams were what she thought were needed to win my affections. Not true, not true at all. By marrying Charlotte I found, until her death, a wonderful partner for forty-five years, a lover, and a fellow social justice activist. Our problems were mostly centered on how to raise our children.

Charlotte was a strong person; a charismatic leader; and a loving, caring, devoted wife, mother, and grandmother with many other wonderful (and much less wonderful) tendencies and characteristics.

After withstanding the various and often intensely hostile reactions from our families, we looked for and found a way to get married. We decided to have the ceremony at City Hall.

An African American couple was also getting married that day. They had witnesses, but we didn't, so I asked them to be our witnesses, and they willingly agreed. We had a surprisingly solemn and traditional ceremony officiated by a well-trained and experienced employee of the city clerk. In that we married so quickly after the joyous engagement party, we didn't see a need to invite our friends to our simple service. We also couldn't think of any family members who would have been comfortable attending.

We were newlyweds out of work, but I had some savings, and we moved into the Albert Hotel. We enjoyed almost every day we lived at this almost-anything-goes residence at University Place and Tenth Street. (Management practices were tightened after we left.) For an interracial couple married in 1953, that Greenwich Village neighborhood was an island of acceptance.

We knew, however, that we were embarking on a voyage without a pilot light, but burning within us was a laser-like determination to make this most improbable, taboo-defying marriage work.

Before facing that realty, we wanted to have a fun-filled and adventuresome first year. We certainly did. As people tended to share with Charlotte and me parts of their lives they were likely to keep from others, we met fascinating, exotic outliers of society who let us into their wonderlands.

One such experience began soon after we settled in. We met three short Jewish men and a tall, in-resident prostitute working independently. The men appeared to be in their mid-fifties and the woman in her mid-thirties.

I will call them, Aaron, Josh, Hesh, and Ellen. Aaron lived a quiet, determined, and dignified life writing Yiddish literary novellas. His hotel roommate was Josh, who dared not bother Aaron but centered his life on taking advantage of other people. Hesh, who lived in the North Bronx, was a naïve communist whom Josh could fool again and again.

The men befriended Ellen, who was quite proud of her professional abilities. When I asked her how she dealt with men when she didn't want to be bothered, she said the trick was to scare them off by telling them, "Do not sabotage me."

Josh convinced Hesh to take the three of them to nightclubs and bars. Then one day Ellen announced that she was pregnant. No one thought the father was Aaron, Josh, or Hesh. Within a month or two, Ellen called Charlotte and me to her room. She wanted me to deliver the baby. I told her I couldn't possibly do that.

Luckily a nurse practitioner resided on the floor. She took a look at Ellen and immediately arranged for an ambulance to Saint Vincent, a nearby Catholic Hospital, where she soon gave birth. When we visited Ellen, we learned that the nuns were exasperated. She only wanted to eat frankfurters and drink cokes. She told us that she arranged with the nuns to give the baby up for adoption.

We then learned that Hesh took her into his nicely furnished apartment in the Amalgamated Housing co-op, a socialist-inspired enclave in the Gun Hill section of the Bronx. When Hesh told us about this, he said, "She will eat normal food, live in a normal place, be with normal people, and will become normal." What happened was far from normal. In a matter of weeks, Hesh told us that Ellen was servicing her clients in his apartment and allowing Hesh to watch.

Now that I think about it, Aaron may have put up with Josh so he could have grist for his novellas.

One of the reasons I selected this story was that it reminded me so much of conversations I had while in college with Marxists who would insist that come the revolution, people would no longer have to smoke, steal and or become a prostitute.

As Charlotte and I matured, we avoided such bizarre encounters, but some people continued to reveal to us their most protected secrets and to invite us to enter into and share a minichapter in their lives.

I considered the idea of starting a support group for interracial couples. Those we met, however, either didn't get along with each other or didn't want to think of themselves as interracial. Nevertheless, we learned some things from that experience. One of the couples we spoke to bought a house in a white neighborhood in Queens, New York, and it was not long before a cross was burned on their lawn. We went to visit them and learned that the mayor at the time, Vincent R. Impellitteri, took strong action. He sent the police to investigate and issued a statement that such behavior would not be tolerated.

Knowing the mayor had protected an interracial couple, we did not hesitate to call on the police for help when we needed it. We made such a call when the next place we moved to was in an all-white neighborhood and the custodian would not give us our mailbox key. I had suggested that we move there because the rents were low, and I knew the area as it was near where I used to live.

The custodian was probably reacting angrily to several pressures: orders from the owner of the building, angry criticisms from tenants, and especially to the ploy I used to get the apartment. I had asked one of our white friends to come with me when I wanted to see whether the apartment was still available. Therefore the custodian didn't know that he was going to be renting to a couple of "troublemakers."

After being refused our key, Charlotte and I went to the police station and told them our story. Without hesitation the officers sped to our building, arrived before we did, and made sure that we would receive our key. When the custodian handed it to me, he let me know that I had caused him a lot of trouble. I told him, "If you have any more trouble, I know a good lawyer who could help you." He replied, "Never mind, you made enough trouble for me already." He never bothered us again.

One of the residents was so upset when she saw us moving in that she fell down the stairs and broke one of her limbs. We began to think that we would be the cause of accidents whenever we showed up unexpectedly.

We had a good marriage and often felt wonderful that we could take on challenges, over and over again, and survive and thrive. We often waded into unchartered waters, however, and only recognized our mistakes after we saw how hurtful we had been to each other. In some respects we refused to learn and change. Despite those instances we usually found a way to resolve our differences or to find separate ways to satisfactorily address them.

I learned and I am still learning about the meaning of our life together. Maybe it came down to what a friend said to me then—a friend whom I had not seen since I was fourteen years old. While Charlotte and I were living in this all-white and mostly Jewish neighborhood in the Bronx, this friend, now a pharmacist, worked across the street from our apartment building. He said to me, "Abe, you and your wife are teaching us all how to become more accepting of each other."

These words were not what I expected. He was one of the older boys I grew up with who mistreated me often. It was 1954, and we were receiving praise as role models, a rare occurrence in the early years of our marriage!

Only one man in the entire building complex spoke to us in the year and a half that we lived on Walton Street. He did so willingly and openly on the street, defying anyone to say or do anything nasty to us. Curiously, he was fervently prejudiced against Puerto Ricans, who at that time were coming to New York in masses. In contrast, he accepted us with seemingly open arms but once told us that the Puerto Ricans "are the worst people on Earth."

I don't think I argued with him, but I learned soon after that to speak up when I heard such outright bigotry. I would ask anyone who made bigoted statements, "How many Puerto Ricans or members of another ethnic or racial group have you met? And so, how can you accurately speak about them?"

So, with only a couple of exceptions, we faced an implacably biased, unfriendly, and cold group of neighbors, and I began to wonder why I had wanted to move there. I still wonder about that to this day. Was it to show Charlotte the kind of people I grew up with? Was it a way to show people like my family that we were a strong, successful couple? Or was it just to have a very good place to live with low rents? (We paid $52 a month for a furnished one-bedroom apartment.)

Maybe it was for all those reasons and more, but we knew we wanted to live again with neighbors who were not shocked every time we appeared in public. So, it was with a great sense of relief and enthusiasm that we moved back to the far more openly accepting Greenwich Village.

It wasn't long, however, after moving into a well-designed and cared-for private apartment complex on Perry Street that some of the Greenwich Villagers displayed their true feelings. I was sent a message to come to the management office, and when I arrived, the person in charge said he wanted to see our marriage license. I said angrily, "I will show it to you before a judge in court!" Charlotte and I never heard from the manager again.

Three

SHOCK, RAGE, BIGOTRY, PAIN, JOY, AND GROWTH

1952

Charlotte opened a letter from her father and was shocked on reading, "Every Cochran and Sewell, living or dead, would strongly oppose you marrying a white man." (Sewell was her mother's maiden name.)

My family first learned of my relationship with Charlotte when a first cousin saw us walking near Forty-Second Street. I didn't notice her, and she didn't say anything to us, but she certainly told my parents.

I was taken by surprise when my father arrived at Irvington House in his Buick with my two sisters and my brother Milton's wife Gladys, who assumed the role of the family's spokesperson. My father insisted that I join them in the car. They then tried to make me feel like I was doing the worst thing I could possibly do in life. Gladys said it would be more acceptable if I married a Chinese woman. She was the most status-conscious of anyone in the family. They offered to introduce me to a white woman. I listened, but I let them know I was going ahead with the marriage.

When my father heard this, he said with fury in his voice, "This is not going to happen." Believe it or not, this was the first time in my life that my father tried to stop me from doing something that I really wanted to do. I can still hear the anger ringing in his voice!

A few days later, my two sisters and Gladys sent word to Charlotte that they wanted to have a talk with her. Charlotte let them know that she would have "none of that." In response, my mother threatened to die of a heart attack. She also told me that my brother, Sidney, thought I should be seen at the psychiatric ward at Bellevue Hospital. I called Sidney and told him, "Keep the hell out of my life." My sister Esther said she was concerned that our children would have a really hard time, and my sister Marsha said that I was having sex for the first time and that's why I wanted to marry Charlotte.

My brother Milton, on the other hand, suggested that I live with Charlotte for one year. If we still loved each other and wanted to get married, he would accept the marriage. I told Milton that it was going to be hard to get by with a marriage license, never mind living together as husband and wife without one.

After we were married I visited my family without Charlotte. The experience was very uncomfortable. They talked about everything but our marriage. It was then that I vowed never to visit again if Charlotte was not welcomed to come with me.

I refused to tell my father where I lived or worked. I did not want to be harassed by him or the family. Nevertheless, he always found me. He would plead with me to visit. One time, I lost my temper and told him to leave me alone and that I was no longer his son.

Soon after the wedding, Charlotte's father — upon meeting me at Charlotte's beloved Uncle Bob's house in Long Island—changed his attitude. I found him to be warm and accepting. On the other hand, when Charlotte's mother visited, she was formal and asked to see our marriage license, and I begrudgingly showed it to her.

Later, during the first year of our marriage, we visited Atlanta. We traveled by train, and when it stopped in DC, we were told that for the remainder of the trip we would have to sit in separate cars. I was shocked, but we did not make an issue of it. On arriving in Atlanta, Charlotte's father (despite not feeling well) and grandfather met us and drove us in separate cars to the family house so that we would not be seen together. It was feared that we might face harassment, rejection by cab drivers, or physical assault.

After worrying about that on the drive home from the airport, the family treated us warmly. Although we arrived about five a.m., Charlotte's mother had a delicious breakfast prepared for us with mini sausages, Canadian bacon, and hot buns.

During our weeklong stay, we were taken to see modern Atlanta, highlighted by the well-known Omni, a hotel and sports arena complex located downtown: a glass structure with see-through elevators attached to the outer walls of buildings situated within a huge and magnificent atrium.

On another day, Charlotte's mother and Aunt Ethel drove us through block after block of homes owned by members of the black upper middle class. They were not only spectacular but objects of intense competition. It was as if their owners were in a race to see who could be more closely identified with the whites of high social and economic status. Believe it or not, one of the homes had a beautiful little boat embedded snugly on the roof.

Most memorable, however, was when Charlotte's grandfather and I were sitting on rocking chairs facing a fireplace with a steady, calming flame. He showed me a newspaper clipping of his becoming the first black to be selected for a jury, and while rocking gently, we shared other stories about ourselves. He spoke of having a successful career as an insurance agent. I spoke of my interest in social work, and just as I started talking about my curiosity about the wonders of the universe, Ethel's son John walked in.

He overheard me talking about the dynamics of the atom. John was eight years old, and he said he knew about the subject. As he spoke it became obvious that he was making things up. When I tried to correct him, and he refused to accept my explanation, Charlotte's grandmother, Eula Sewell, the empirical matriarch of the family, who had entered the room when she heard John's voice, told him emphatically to be quiet.

We also visited the part of the family that Charlotte loved dearly. They were hardworking, very warm and accepting, and they went out of their way to help each other. Of those we met, no one had gone to college. Yet, several had good jobs that required a high level of intelligence and skills. One of the cousins, Billie Pinkney, for example, was a mechanic on state-of-the-art air force planes.

During our conversations Charlotte loved the fact that they weren't in the least bit arrogant, and neither did they need to convince anyone that they deserved a higher status than other blacks. Robert Pinkney and his wife who everyone lovingly called Pete were the parents of the large extended family. They were in their late eighties when I met them. Robert told me he was related to Charlotte's grandmother, Eula Sewell, and that he had left her super-controlling ways and home in his teens to become a roustabout, one who goes from town to town trying to find work.

Robert and I formed a warm relationship. When he beat me consistently in dominos, I teased him, saying that he was not playing according to my rules. He would respond, "Abe, you play by Brooklyn rules, and they are wrong." My fondness for Robert extended to his children and to his grandchildren, who have remained close to this day and especially to my son and his family.

When we returned to Charlotte's parents' home to get ready for the trip back to New York, her father reported that he had just seen a doctor, and his blood pressure was very high. I suggested that he rest and maybe someone else accompany Charlotte to the train station. He said no, he would do it.

Later that year, Charlotte was sent word that her father died. She was told that it might be better if I didn't come for the funeral. I decided I wanted to be with her at this terribly sad time. Without much money we decided to take a low-cost "charter" flight.

Within a half hour of flight, the plane was caught in a fierce storm and was forced to land in Washington, DC. We were told that we would get an Eastern Air Lines flight in the morning, but that we would have to find a place to stay overnight. We trudged from one black-owned motel to another, soaking wet, and were turned away. After a long, exhaustive search, we finally found a black motel owner who allowed us to stay.

Once in Atlanta, Charlotte's aunt told me it was a mistake for me to come as they could be bombed for housing a white man. So while everyone went to the funeral I stayed hidden and alone in the Cochran home.

Four years into our marriage, our first child, a daughter, Chandelle ("Chandy") was born. In taking her home from the hospital and holding her in my arms, I had what may be a universal feeling, but to me this precious little body whose bones lay gently in my arms was wondrous and thrilling to behold.

We found her name in my old French/English textbook. It means candle. Our Jewish diaper man startled us when he heard her name. He said her name means Sheyndela (a pretty little girl.)

Shortly after her birth, both of our mothers happened to visit us at the same time. They seemed relaxed with each other. When I was accepted into social work school, my parents gave us forty dollars a month.

After we were married seven years, my mother and father moved into their own apartment. They moved from Townsend Avenue further west to Burnside Avenue near the Grand Concourse. I am not sure why they moved away from the family's apartment. Maybe they wanted us to visit without criticism from my two sisters. Maybe they didn't want their three grandchildren to know about our marriage. Maybe they didn't want to face sharp criticism and rejection from their longtime neighbors on Townsend Avenue. Maybe it was the status of living nearer to the Grand Concourse. Maybe it was to lessen some of my mother's burden in caring for three families in one apartment.

To our surprise, after they moved, they invited Charlotte and me for dinner a couple of times. On these visits my mother was particularly relaxed. Even her cooking, which was sometimes tasteless when I was a child, was now quite delicious.

Unfortunately, this wonderful period came to an end. Against Charlotte's fierce objection, I took a social work job in Seattle, Washington. I wanted the job because it was working with "pre-delinquent youth." I thought it would be the kind of group work experience that matched my training but was not available in New York. It was, I believed, an opportunity to serve where I could make a real difference.

My parents were furious. My father sent very angry letters, accusing Charlotte of taking me away from them. I tried to explain, without success, that it was my idea to move to Seattle. I should have met with my parents before we left to explain why I wanted this job. I am not sure why I didn't think of doing that. It wasn't until we came back from Seattle that my father would listen to my explanation for having gone.

Charlotte was very unhappy in Seattle, even though we found great friends. In desperation, I promised her that after two years, if she still wanted so badly to be back in New York, we would return, which we did.

After returning from Seattle, and nine years into my marriage, my father and I had still not reconciled. I began to feel I had not done enough to reach out to him. I felt that with my training in social work, there should be some way to talk openly about my marriage and my actions. I thought of taking him on walks like those he took me on years ago.

Before raising the subject, I asked about my mother, who suffered for many years with diabetes and was very ill and in the hospital. I had visited her a few days before, and she was warm toward me but looked quite weak. Pop spoke of how terrible it was that she was suffering so much.

After a pause I asked him why it was so hard for him to accept Charlotte. I was surprised that he revealed that now that it looked like my mother was going to die, he wished one of Charlotte's African American female friends would live with and take care of him. It wasn't in the form of a request. It sounded like he was telling me that he could now be more accepting of Charlotte and the marriage.

A few weeks later, my mother died, and he asked to meet me. To my amazement he proudly stated, "Abie, we shall overcome!" It was right after President Johnson used that phrase in the process of passing the Voting Rights Bill. Then my father said, "I want Charlotte to come to Momma's funeral."

In the funeral parlor before the burial ceremony, and without Charlotte present, Esther, with me and all the rest of my family present, gave my father a tongue-lashing. She called him stupid and asked him, "Do you know the gantse mishpokhe are coming. Do you think they want their children to marry into a family with someone who is black?" (gantse mispokhe means the whole family, including the soon-to-be in-laws of the grown children planning to get married.)

My brother Milton spoke up in forceful words in support of my father. He said, "Papa is not stupid. Abie and Charlotte have a good marriage, and Charlotte is coming to the funeral."

Sidney came up to me and, in a warm tone, said that this kind of family hassle was not good. Gladys let it be known that she was in agreement with Milton.

Although we felt somewhat wary, Charlotte and I went to the funeral, and Charlotte was pleased that some family members were quite relaxed with her. Relationships with the rest of the family gradually improved.

Taking a ten-year momentary leap forward to 1974, shortly after my father died, Esther, who was administrator of my father's estate, sent Charlotte and me a note. Enclosed was a two-hundred-dollar check. She wrote, "I think Pop would have liked each of his grandchildren to have this. Best wishes, Esther."

Twenty years after that, in 1994, when we were babysitting with our first grandchild, Tariq, Esther and Manny visited and were warm toward the baby and cordial to Charlotte and me.

It is important to note that my nephew Paul (Esther and Manny's son), in his own quiet way, accepted our marriage from day one. He visited us well before anyone else was ready. He would tell me of weddings and funerals and asked if I would have wanted to attend any of them. I always said yes, if Charlotte was also invited. Because of my father's growth and courage, Paul didn't have to ask me that question when my mother died.

Two other people who were there for us at the beginning of our marriage were Jeanne "Jennie" Laefer, my father's niece, and her husband, Joe. They invited Charlotte and me to their home for dinner soon after we married. What took us all by surprise was when my aunt, Jennie's mother, Gussie, who was my father's older sister, saw Charlotte and me together, and she started screaming at everyone. Joe escorted her out of the room, and Jennie apologized.

That was some of what we contended with during the first years of our marriage.

Four

WHAT I LEARNED AS A BABY

Charles Lindbergh on May 20–21, 1927 on the first nonstop flight from New York to Paris, won the $25,000 Outeig Prize.

—WIKIPEDIA

Whenever I am asked where I was born, I often tell people I was smart enough at the age of six months to move out of Brooklyn and into the Bronx. But that is not really an example of bias against Brooklyn. It is just my attempt at a joke. In fact, I have always thought people from Brooklyn tended to have more warmth than residents of the other boroughs. But I am open to argument on that score. My deepest biases and attitudes, however, did, as mentioned earlier, become imbedded during my infancy and my earliest years. Although it would be hard to find out now what I experienced as a Brooklynite during my initial months of life outside the womb, as I got a little older, living on Ward Avenue in the Bronx, I made, without realizing it, many observations regarding race: Only white people lived in the nice houses that lined both sides of our street. Only white children attended my school and played on our street. Only white people came to visit us in our home. When I was allowed to go to the movies, I noticed that it was only white people who performed heroic acts, while the few blacks on screen were enslaved, ridiculed, or assigned the lowest status and most demeaning roles.

According to Shankar Vedantam in his book, *The Hidden Brain*, my reality was the norm for a white child. Although this is changing, it remains the norm in many neighborhoods around the country. Vedantam writes that the type of experiences I had leads to a favorable bias toward whites and a negative bias against people of color, *regardless of parental influences.*

Until about the age of nine, or around 1935, I do not recall ever seeing a person of color on our block. Then an important incident occurred. I had a desire to help my mother with her endless chores. Besides taking care of our large family in our ground-floor, seven-room apartment, she oversaw the maintenance of the entire three-family house that my parents owned.

I was in the basement with her as she was tending the coal pile outside the stove that was used to heat the entire building. It was a delivery day, and the blue-black chunks were tumbling down a coal truck chute through the basement window. The man tending to the free flow of coal was dark-skinned. He was quite relaxed with us. He told us how hard it was to grow up in the South and that he had to walk to school, often through deep snow for a very long distance with holes in his shoes. I remember my mother showing interest by listening carefully. I do not remember speaking, but I was very impressed by his story.

The only times I saw people of color fairly often was when my parents visited relatives who lived in a poorer section in the heart of the South Bronx. My two aunts, my mother's sisters, and their families lived in the same tenement in separate apartments on the fifth floor. It was on Dawson Street near Intervale and Westchester Avenues. The entire block had only walk-up tenements.

Only blacks lived on the lower half of Dawson Street. Only whites lived on the upper half, and my aunts' building was at the dividing point. It was the first of the whites-only buildings adjoining the last of the blacks-only buildings.

I always looked forward to visiting my aunts so I could play with my cousin, also named Abe, who was about nine months younger than me. One early evening, when we were eight and nine years old, we found a way to get into my father's car. We imagined that we were driving. One of us accidentally released the brakes, and because of the downward slant of the street, the car rolled into the car in front of us. Some black kids who were standing on the sidewalk and who witnessed it made angry gestures toward us and then ran into their building. I assumed it was to tell the owner of the car what we had done. We were very frightened, scampered out of the car, and ran into my aunts' building and up the stairs to let my father know what happened.

Pop came down as fast as he could as a group of black adults were gathering around the cars. He jumped into his car and sped off at high speed. I don't remember whether or not he came back for us that night.

One time, after that, I remember being very frightened upon climbing the stairs to see my cousins when a black man was right behind me. The fact that he gave me a friendly smile didn't alleviate my fear.

In short, what became imbedded in my brain was a variety of attitudes and stereotypes: the hidden or implicit biases of white privilege and the belief that blacks were inferior and to be feared.

At the same time, I admired black people for their strength in dealing with bigotry and poverty. My negative attitudes were reinforced by family members expressing prejudicial characterizations of people of color, but they were countered by having been impressed by the coal man's warmth and his compelling story.

I have two other strong but nonracial childhood memories. The first one was when my oldest brother, Milty, without asking me in advance, gave me an adorable beagle hound pup. I was probably about seven or eight years old. I loved the dog and called him Pal. In the spring we kept him tied up in our front-yard garden.

I felt sorry that he was not free to roam about. So, when I came home from school, I would untie him, and he would run up the street, looking for other dogs to be with.

One day, without telling me, my family gave Pal away to the large Italian family living across the street. I was told that they had a large farm upstate where Pal could roam without being tied up for hours.

I remember going off by myself and crying. I grieved for Pal for quite a long time. As the youngest in the family, it was thought that I didn't have the judgment to be involved even in a decision that affected me the most. That is why I tell those close to me — even to this day —that if they want my help or participation in a project, I will be more considerate if I am invited to participate in the planning stage.

What added salt to my wound was when the son of the family that took Pal — who was a few years older than me — stole my bicycle and painted it to hide the fact that it was mine. My family didn't do anything about it, and I did not muster the courage to confront the thief by myself.

The second experience occurred when I was about nine. There was an older boy who bullied me in the schoolyard. One day the bully was in the yard at the same time as me and Milty. I asked my brother to speak to him. Rather than do that, Milty thought I should go over and tell the boy that he should stop bothering me.

Despite being scared and angry that my brother was not aware of how scared I was, I approached the boy. I do not remember what I said, but it worked. He never bothered me again.

Marsha, Pop, Esther and me.

Five

THE HILL OUTSIDE MY KITCHEN WINDOW

1930s

Cost of a first-class stamp: $0.02

The adoption of children of one race by parents of another race—began officially in the United States in 1948

—*WIKIPEDIA*

Ours was a Jewish household, and we lived in the East Bronx. My racial attitudes in my preteens were an extension of those I developed as a child. There were still no blacks on my block or any of the surrounding blocks in my neighborhood. There were no blacks in my school. The racially charged incident that occurred in front of my aunts' building five years earlier took place several miles south of our home.

In the early years of my childhood, there were miles of open spaces and two farms across unpaved Eastern Boulevard. Today, it is called Bruckner Boulevard, one of the main thoroughfares in the Bronx, bordering for endless miles on our former fun-filled, open fields. It is now covered with bricks and pipes sunk into our sandlots and grassy fields to support modern housing and stores.

Life for a young child was so different than it is today. We could play out-side all day without parental supervision. No questions were asked as long as we came home to eat and sleep. Our house on Ward Avenue was the last one on the block. It adjoined a magic hill. During the rainy season, newly formed ponds would appear at the bottom of its steepest side. We fell over each other and into the water trying to catch the most worms. In the summer we would sit between a huge, split stone outgrowth and imagine we were airplane cap-tains on dangerous missions. In the winter, we would take turns sleigh-riding down the hill. Everyone would line up in a row along the path of the down-ward slide and pile on one at a time as the sled approached. By the time we reached the bottom, four or five of us were layered on top of each other, grab-bing on desperately. We wanted to see how many could stay on before the sled reached the bottom. Often we fell off on the way down and would start over again until we were too wet to stay outdoors.

When looking outside my kitchen window, if I saw my friends on the hill, I would often join them. We would play cowboys and Indians, cops and rob-bers, and we even built a wooden "hideout" in plain view on the very top of the hill. But nothing in our imaginary play could compare to a real incident.

We had periodic snowball fights with the "foreign" kids from over the hill on Manor Avenue. They were about our age, and once we got to know them, we found out that they were also Jewish and lived in homes almost identical to ours.

Across the street from the hill, we built snow forts on our block. We armed ourselves with a mountain of snowballs. The Manor Avenue Boys would charge down the hill with ready-made snowballs, and we would bombard them with ours. Most of the time you could not tell who won and who lost. One day, however, our marksmanship overwhelmed our "enemies," and they ran back to their street, soaking wet and humbled in defeat.

We didn't have much time to celebrate our military victory when we looked up the hill and saw their big brothers running toward us with ven-geance in their eyes. They picked us up, turned us upside down, and dropped us headfirst into our snow forts.

With time, our battles morphed into stickball games. When we visited the Manor Avenue Boys on their turf, we were astonished. They played all the games we played, and we didn't know how they had learned them. How could they possibly have learned the games that we had invented?

Slowly, it occurred to us that we didn't invent these games: stoop, curve and slug ball, pitcher-batter-catcher, ringolevio, Johnny-on-the-pony, kick the can, and many others. It finally dawned on us that these were games that many other kids knew and loved as much as we did.

Ringolevio was our favorite featuring capture, rescue, running, and evading war. Years later I saw a painting by Pieter Breugal, dated 1560, called "Children Playing." He could have painted it on Ward Avenue in the 1930s. It illustrated many of the same games we played. Who knew?

One rare pick-up game with boys from a few surrounding blocks made a lasting impression. Two boys chose players to be on their side from among kids from more than one block. For the first time, I was picked to play on a team on which I was the oldest. I soon found that I could also hit the ball farther than anyone else. When I helped my team win, I reveled in the unfamiliar praise that followed.

For years before, when I was the youngest among my teammates, the Ward Avenue Window-Breakers, I had been humiliated by them over and over again because I couldn't play as well as they did. Several times when we just hit the ball to each other, and it was my time to bat, my so-called friends would say it was too hot to keep playing. They would take their gloves, bats, and balls and, without so much as a good-bye, go home. I didn't say anything, but it hurt me very much. Nevertheless, it added to the emotional pain I experienced at home. In essence, however, the unsupervised play, both harsh and wholesome, was a good preparation for what I faced all through my life.

On writing this book I gained a new insight. What the Ward Avenue Window-Breakers experienced before visiting the Manor Avenue Boys was an observation that anthropologists believe is close to universal: Groups or tribes that are isolated from others develop myths idolizing their own abilities, considering themselves unique or exceptional while believing other tribes are inferior. We actually thought we invented those games, and when we met the

Manor Avenue Boys, we thought we were better than they were. That feeling lasted until their big brothers turned us headfirst into the world of reality.

What added to my sensitivity toward the plight of the underdog—the poor, people of color, and natives of North America—was the anger I felt when my peers took advantage of me for being the youngest.

The Great Depression of the 1930s dominated our lives, and the New Deal programs that helped many blacks also helped whites, including my family. Like many of the homeowners on Ward Avenue, we received help from the Home and Building Loan Association of the New Deal in the purchase of our house.

Like many others who went through those trying days, the strife of the times had a powerful influence on my attitudes toward the precariousness of life. From the ages of nine and ten, I was often sent to the grocer, without money, to ask if my family could be given food and pay later. The grocer always took my list with a slight, knowing smile and filled bags of food, and so I assumed my mother would pay him eventually.

On the other hand, the families that lived on the second floor of our three-family house had a much more difficult time saying yes when I was told to collect the rent from them. Every time I walked up the lonely, narrow flight of stairs, knocked on their doors, and asked them to pay their arrears, they looked annoyed. They seldom made a payment and often moved out without a word to my parents. One family not only didn't pay what they owed, they moved and took with them my father's cherished collection of Enrico Caruso's albums that they had borrowed.

Although Pop didn't tell us why we moved in 1942, I imagine not being able to collect the rents was a major reason. I will never forget how awful my sister Marsha and I felt as my father drove us to our new residence on Stratford Avenue. Although we found it to be a fairly nice tenement farther west in the Bronx, we loved the seven-room house on Ward Avenue. Besides its front garden, garage, and backyard that extended most of the length of Ward Avenue behind a row of about twelve duplicate homes separated by wide alleyways, it was the center of our lives for the main years of our childhood. Whereas the girls were not allowed to play on the streets, we sometimes played with them behind our buildings by racing and skipping rope.

During this time, I became very depressed when I learned that my brother Milton was questioned by the police about a coat that was taken from a department store. Milton was my hero and role model, and I didn't want him to go to jail. I was not told how that was resolved, but he was not arrested.

Regarding my attitude toward spending, I became a steady saver, to such an extent that about sixty years later, members of the family thought I was worth much more than I was in reality. For example, on planning to take Tariq, my grandson, to a Knicks basketball game, I learned that the worst seats, which were farthest from the court, were priced at eighty dollars each. As we entered Madison Square Garden, Tariq and I stepped into the Knicks store to look around, and Tariq wanted me to get him an expensive memento. When I refused and reminded him how much the tickets cost, he blurted out, "Grandpa, you are rich."

The same seats cost six dollars when I took Tariq's father, my son, Michael, and his lifelong friend, Richard, to a basketball game at Madison Square Garden when they were boys. It took me several years to convince Tariq that I was not rich but that I did manage to save what should be enough for my retirement—that is if I don't live forever. So as many Great Depression babies learned, I adopted a habit of saving, which for years before the 2009 Great Recession was considered "quaint."

As Roosevelt took steps to improve job prospects, people started buying costume jewelry again, my father's spirits began to rise, and we were able pay the grocer in a timely manner.

In 1938, as a twelve-year-old earning three dollars a week in a grocery store, I felt that my chance of getting more was good. So I asked my boss for a raise to five dollars a week. He turned me down, so I quit.

My cousin Manny was visiting when I told him and my brother Sidney what happened, and Manny said, "Abie, you should have had another job lined up before you quit."

When my friends reached an age beyond puberty, and I still had a couple of years to wait, they would do things like drag me across the street and force me to talk to a beautiful girl my age. I was embarrassed and couldn't speak.

Then they started to look for girls about ten short blocks away. They weren't sure whether to take me along, but usually they did. One evening an older boy who was new to our crowd, and whose family had moved into one of the apartments in our house on Ward Avenue, waited until we had gotten to the place where we thought the girls would be, and he complained to the others about me, saying, "This little kid should not be here. He will just be in the way. Why the hell did you bring him?" He told me to go home.

I had resented all the attention he had been getting when we played ball. He was quite athletic, well-built, and good-looking. So when he started complaining about my presence, all my repressed anger about being treated badly for years (while the newcomer was favored right after joining us) shot through my body, and I hit him in the face as hard as I could.

I ran away and hid behind bushes in a front-yard garden of a house a few blocks away. I could hear him talking to my friends while they looked for me. I heard him say, "If I catch him, I'll beat the hell out of him." For days after that, he would not come down to play with us, and within a short time, his family moved out. I never told my mother or father that I may have been the cause of their leaving.

I remember times during my childhood when I felt very close to my father. Such times took place when I was about eleven years old. On Saturdays, he would take me with him to check the mail at his costume jewelry–making shop on Seventh Avenue across from Macy's in Manhattan. Afterward he would take me for a bite to eat and to see a movie on Forty-Second Street. I was allowed to pick my favorite hot dog store where they sold two franks or a frank and root beer for a nickel. I would usually choose the latter because I loved root beer. Then we would see a film at the Apollo Theater across the street. We saw some of the greatest foreign films. I loved those trips from the Bronx as I had my father all to myself, and I was introduced to the freer sexual mores in the European cinema. I would still go there in my twenties, and who was more of a sight to behold for a young man's eyes than Gina Lollabrigida!

Six

THE DAY I BECAME A MAN

Cost of a postage stamp in 1939: $0.03 and
There were 32 lynchings of blacks in the 1940s.

Preparations for my Bar Mitzvah ceremony were a mixture of joy and the bizarre. The joy for me was being enrolled in a Jewish Folksschul, learning to read and understand Yiddish, learning the stories of the Bible, and helping younger boys prepare for their big day even before my own day arrived.

The bizarre part started when we were taught, in preparation, to read Hebrew but not to understand it. What totally confused me was that while memorizing the melody, we had to read without knowing what we were reading. Based on our birthday, we were assigned to read either a small number of lines or many pages of the Haftorah (the words of the prophets). It was a colossal stroke of luck when I learned that I was assigned twenty-six lines compared to my friend's twenty-six pages. We felt sorry for him. Whenever we would call on him to play, he could not come out. Having had a traditional upbringing, he was eagerly studying his part.

We all knew that it was a historical anomaly to believe that after reading the bible (in words foreign to us) and giving an original speech (in English) to the congregation (mostly family), that we would be considered full-grown men. These tasks did not convince us that we were actually old enough to accept and be responsible for acting within the moral code of Judaism.

A few days after making my "becoming a man" speech, my father came from work in the late afternoon to meet me as I was leaving shul. He said, "I want to tell you about an agreement I had with Mama about your going to Shul. I did not want you to attend in the first place, but Mama wanted you to not only go but to remain in shul well after your Bar Mitzvah. So, we compromised. I told her I would pay for you to attend until your Bar Mitzvah and not after that."

I was quite surprised and said, "But Papa, I like shul and especially the stories."

He then said, "These stories are just legends, and God didn't create man; man created God."

It took me a little while to fully absorb what he said, but in a few days, I realized that he made sense. Since then I have worked out my own form of belief. I am an agnostic but not as it is usually defined. Whereas most agnostics are not sure whether or not God exists, I am sure that no anthropomorphic superbeing exists.

My religious-like feeling lies in the wonder of how a 13.8-billion-year-old universe so vast, with many unsolved mysteries, could have been self-initiating.

If it was self-initiating, then is there a how and a why?

Seven

***Postage stamps did not exceed 0.06
cents through the 1960s***

*During the 1960s no lynchings as such were recorded.
Lynchings, nonetheless, morphed into other forms of brutal
killings—Emmet Till in 1955 and Chaney, Goodman,
and Schwerner in 1964, among many others.*

UNKNOWN SOURCE

Around the age of sixteen, I went through a period of depression. I wondered if I could kill myself with a knife. When I held one in my hand and looked at it, I realized I could not do it. I told my sisters about it, and they told my father, and he acted quickly.

He walked with me up the magic hill where we were completely alone. He spoke of another person who considered my father a confidante. This man had a wife who was so mentally ill that they did not have a sexual life together. To fulfill his needs, he found a prostitute. Then Pop said that he would be willing to make arrangements for me to meet this prostitute if I was interested.

I told my father that I was not interested as I didn't think it was sex that was bothering me. However, I am not sure to this day what it was. In addition, though I have been frustrated sexually at times and have thought about it for a moment or two, sleeping with a prostitute never appealed to me.

During those days, members of the family offered their designs for my future career. My mother announced at a family gathering that she wanted me to become a pharmacist because a cousin was earning a good living at it. She saw this as a high-status profession. I was somewhat pleased that my mother was thinking about me. However, it seemed odd that she would make a recommendation about me to the family without discussing it with me beforehand, as if it didn't matter what I thought.

My sister-in-law Gladys wanted me to become a printer because her father had owned a very successful printing business, and her uncle earned a good salary as a linotype operator. She thought that there would be good opportunities for me.

At the time I believed that these suggestions were aimed at satisfying my own needs. Looking back, however, I wonder if my mother and Gladys were protecting the earning power of my two brothers who worked with my father in their small business. If they did, they were misjudging me. Consciously I never thought of wanting to work full time in the "business," although I did some selling for the "shop" in my college years. Also, when my brothers were in the army, I worked a whole summer for my father and earned about $700. That was a good amount of money in 1942 for a sixteen-year-old. I saved it, and as mentioned, ten years later, Charlotte and I put it to good use when we started our life together without jobs.

I figured out, later in life, with some help from a therapist, that I tend to pay my bills late, which is possibly due to a hidden feeling of being left out of the family business without being consulted. The decent thing would have been for my family to discuss why it was that only my brothers were expected to partner with my father in the shop, even if my sisters and I were not even talking about that as a possibility.

I did, however, change from an academic high school to a printing vocational school and found a job in a print shop. I enjoyed assisting the proofreader and using one of the printing machines. This was a union shop. For me to become an apprentice, the union representative, who was a senior worker there, had to agree to sponsor me. He kept promising but did not follow up. For a while I was frustrated and didn't know how to approach this quiet, stern-looking man. Whereas others were quite friendly and encouraging, he was neither.

One day, after months of waiting, I asked myself if I really wanted to be a printer for the rest of my working life, and the answer came to me quickly and with certainty -- and it was no, I did not.

It was at that moment that the flame within me was ignited. It was a flame that motivated me over the rest of my life to keep trying to find out who I was, how to grow, how to serve, and how to translate my passions and my ideas into action.

In the meantime, however, while still in high school, when I wasn't sure what career I could choose that could match the burning sensation within me to succeed, I knew it would involve more schooling. So I left the printing school and enrolled in an academic school, the Theodore Roosevelt Evening High School in the Bronx.

In my last year in high school, an African American schoolmate and I became rivals for the affection of a very attractive, white, fairly tall female student. He was handsome, articulate, and taller than me and her. I had two motives for becoming the one she chose: (1) I really liked her; and (2) It felt like the right thing to do to protect her from an interracial relationship.

When the three of us walked away from school together, he spoke of himself in a favorable light. I then tactfully but assertively intervened. I tried to show her that I liked her as well, and she smiled as if to approve. I felt encouraged to continue acting on her behalf. I believed that it was not good for her to have a more than friendly relationship with someone of color. In 1943, at the age of seventeen, I felt very comfortable taking such a stance, and I continued my relationship with her.

I now realize how normal it felt exercising prejudice against a person of color. And since then how much I have struggled to bring my biases under control.

During that year, I joined the 92nd Street YM & WHA with my cousin Abe and our friend Arnie. The "Y" spelled out meant the Young Men's and Women's Hebrew Association. The track coach taught us race walking. He thought I was good enough to race against Olympic champions in the Coney Island handicap walk. He thought I could do well because beginners were given a huge handicap. I really loved race walking, even though when I practiced on the streets, swinging my hips like a women of the night, onlookers had fun with, "Aren't you cute?" or "Please slow down so we can get together." I would just smile at them and kept walking.

Race walking involves your whole body, and it is rhythmic. I believed it would be my passport to walk my way through old age rather than continually warming a bench.

As I approached my eighteenth birthday, in 1944, I spent time thinking about the Nazis. I fantasized visiting an army prison and being allowed to talk to a German army officer of high rank who was thoroughly imbued with the Nazi ideology. I believed that I would be fully capable of persuading him to change his beliefs. Where that kind of overconfidence came from, I do not know. Years later, after training as a social group worker and after many years working with young adults with firmly fixed ideas, I pride myself (and have been recognized by others) as able to dissuade many men and some women from a wide variety of self-destructive behaviors.

As I became more and more aware of, and more and more furious at, evidence of Nazi atrocities, I decided to join the armed services in advance of being drafted. When I told my track coach, he was upset because I would miss the Coney Island Handicap. Years later, at the age of fifty and having done at least a half hour of walking most days of the week since my days at the Y, I wished I could have met my coach to tell him how much his training meant to me.

I wanted to serve in the merchant marines. I thought it was the most adventuresome because of its coastal stops in exotic foreign lands while requiring great courage volunteering to be easy targets for enemy submarines, ships, and planes. In order to pass the test, however, color recognition was required, and I was red and green deficient. That ability was crucial because the merchant marines used an array of colored flags to communicate with other ships at sea.

I found a doctor who said he could teach me to distinguish colors even though I would not be able see them as most people do. The method would mean observing samples of reds and greens and mixtures of both repeatedly until I could identify them correctly without actually seeing them as most people do.

I decided that this would be too hard and risky. Instead, I took and failed the test for the air force, and joined the army. My army experience was short, only about six months due to a medical discharge. I left just when my battalion was preparing to counter the German attack in the Battle of the Bulge. According to Wikipedia, many US soldiers were killed, and I may be alive today because of a minor medical condition. I had boils on my back to such an extent that it was determined that I couldn't carry the required heavy backpacks.

The boils were caused by the large quantities of gravy put on our potatoes and meats. I should have told the servers, my fellow soldiers, not to pour so much of the greasy sauce on my food, as I had a severe case of acne in civilian life and knew that gravy aggravated the condition. The boils on my back were, in essence, a severe form of acne.

I felt guilty and sought out the Protestant chaplain and said, "I do not believe in the divinity of Jesus but in his humaneness. As you know of his wisdom, can you advise me as to whether I should ask for a hearing?" I don't remember his words, but it felt like I could accept the discharge without feeling guilty.

I sometimes wonder, however, whether some of my unconscious guilt remains. I wonder whether it is that guilt that allows me to take on behavior that others would deem dangerous: finding a way to remove dangerous drug dealers living in my building; or standing up to militant black construction workers in the Bronx who took over our Settlement House office; or an extremist wing of the Black Panthers who wanted to take over the East Harlem youth center that I directed.

During my army basic training I became aware of the explicit anti-Semitism in the South as it occurred in two incidents.

In the first, I was told to go to battalion headquarters to see the master sergeant. He held a letter from the Y. They were returning part of my membership fee. The sergeant asked me, in an accusatory manner, if indeed I was a Hebrew. I said, "Yes, you can call me a Hebrew or a Jew because that is what I am."

To let everyone know I was not ashamed of being Jewish, I decided to line up in front of my barracks whenever the rabbi scheduled a meeting of the Jewish soldiers. I did it even though I was not a practicing Jew, and I was the only one to appear.

Another way to show that I wouldn't be intimidated was to join the boxing tournament. I had boxed a little in the Y and realized I had a powerful punch. I believe the strength in my arms came from the summer I worked with my father, casting low-value jewelry over a tall, wide pot filled with an ultra-heated alloy several hours a day.

Our lieutenant became interested in this fight as a way of challenging the other battalion. He was charismatic and well respected by all the soldiers. He told me, "If you win, I will do twenty pushups in front of the entire battalion." It felt good to have his backing. He had such a commanding presence that I would have followed him no matter what he ordered me to do.

Then some soldiers, very experienced working with boxers, came to my corner and asked if they could be my "seconds," or my manager and my aides. I won the first fight easily, and the writer for the base newspaper wrote that I had a powerful punch and won by a TKO (technical knockout). I kept asking the lieutenant to do the pushups he promised, but he delayed until one day when the entire battalion was training in the woods; he did them quickly and effortlessly.

I also won the next fight with the same "seconds" gladly willing to help. The day before the third fight that would determine the camp's champion for my weight division, middleweight, between 160 and 168 pounds. I was introduced to my opponent. He was superbly built and told me he was the sparring partner for Willy Pepp, one of the greatest boxers of all time, and that he would be seeking a career in boxing when the war ended. I realized that this meeting was set up to frighten me. I do not remember being frightened, but I was thoroughly aware that I had little chance of winning.

On the night of the fight, some men I didn't know came to me and volunteered to be my "seconds." They kept telling me to be the aggressor, to come in close and try to knock my opponent down early in the fight. I followed their advice, though this is not what you tell an amateur when he is fighting a professional. In those circumstances you should box at a distance and hope your opponent gets arm weary trying to hit you. As a result I was beaten badly. In fact, the next day, the corporal who was readying us for a long training march allowed me to go back to the barracks and sleep.

The "seconds" who helped me during the first two fights sought me out and asked me why I allowed this other team to be in my corner to assist me instead of them. I then realized that I was the victim of a scam. To aid my opponent's career potential in boxing, his backers made sure he not only would win, but win decisively. Nonetheless, he didn't knock me out. The third round ended, and I was still on my feet. Even though I lost, no one ever asked me again if I was Jewish.

So for several years afterward, I would tell people, "I won a silver medal boxing in the army, but don't ask me why I didn't win the gold medal." Partly as a result of that experience, I oppose boxing as well as football and hockey that embrace violence.

The next time I became aware of anti-Semitism was when my brother-in-law, who was in the air force, was assigned to my own base at Fort Bragg, North Carolina. He drove down from New York with his wife, my sister Marsha, and because she knew that I loved bagels, she brought some for me. Even though the one I chose to eat was close to rock-hard, I chewed away at it with pleasure.

A day or two later, I visited my sister on the base, and she told me that when she rented the apartment, the landlady asked if she was Jewish. When Marsha told her that she was Jewish, the woman told her in all seriousness that she thought that all Jews had horns and that she was pleased that Marsha had none!

When I arrived home from the service, my family was glad to see me. My brothers were still in the military and served for four years. Milton became a cook and then a military policeman. Sidney was in the air force, assigned to repair large troop carriers.

While in the army, I corresponded with the girl I had met in high school who had also been courted by the young black man and thought that we would go together when I got home. We met, and I was disappointed. She had grown quite heavy, talked about her father's and her own support of Israel, and I felt she was testing whether I felt the same. I had not at that time made up my mind about Israel, and it became clear that she was not interested in continuing our relationship.

Later, while in college, I wrote a poem about my feelings about the Jewish state. The only words I remember are, "Seek not a single haven, ye Jews." Despite my reservations, there is little doubt that the creation of a successful democracy during Israel's early years radically reduced anti-Semitism in the United States. In the later years, however, its military occupation of the West Bank in defiance of the United Nations has led to a worldwide increase in bias toward Jews.

Furthermore, people around the world in recent and ancient history have deeply resented the belief of many Jews that they are special in the eyes of God. This has led to arrogance and elitism and has elicited the enmity of many tribes and nations.

I do not excuse the Islamic nations, Hamas, and others for their unrelenting unwillingness to negotiate with Israel. I believe, however, that Israel needs to take actions, like reversing the spread of settlements. This might convince non-Israelis that they sincerely want peace in the region.

Going back to my experience as a member of the Ward Avenue Window-Breakers and our superior attitude toward the Manor Avenue Boys, the "War" we fought over it, and the fact that there is almost a universal attitude of superiority and exceptionalism of each tribe, nation, and religion toward one another, when will we wake up and realize that it is impossible for all separately to be favored more by God or chance than all the others?

When I was nineteen, we were all living in one apartment. Ten of us shared the five-room apartment on Townsend Avenue. I loved playing with my nephews, Paul and Leonard, and a niece, Paul's little sister, Maxine. These were the children of my two sisters. I made up stories with many chapters for them. I bought a wire recorder, and Maxine and I had much fun recording and playing games. When Leonard was less than two years old, I helped him to take his first steps.

Looking back, it was this experience with the three children and the recommendation of my college social group work professor that convinced me to seek a master's degree in social group work. I specialized in serving children and youth attending community centers, Ys, and settlement houses.

When I joined the service, my high school approved my graduation, though there were a few required courses I hadn't taken. Despite that fact, and despite having only a 73 percent average in high school, I was accepted into the City College of New York (CCNY) as a nonmatriculated student, where the entrance average for nonveteran students was 88 percent.

In those days, CCNY had no tuition, and with the GI Bill, I had enough money to buy all my books and pay my fees. What I didn't expect was how some of the teachers treated those of us who were in their classrooms and barely able to compete. I learned quickly that the faculty considered CCNY the poor man's Harvard, and they let us know that. For example, my English teacher read one of my assignments to the rest of the class as an example of a "D minus" paper.

My trigonometry professor gave us a difficult assignment that I tried hard to solve. At the next few sessions of the course, he would ask if anyone knew how to solve it. I put my hand up every time, and he acted like he didn't see it. I finally spoke up and said I could solve the problem. He was skeptical but allowed me to come up to the blackboard, and I wrote out the solution. He was surprised, and I felt great.

In regard to the English teacher, later in the semester, he asked us to turn in a paper after researching an issue and that it would be acceptable to seek help in writing it as long as it was our idea and that we ourselves wrote the draft.

I read that Einstein described some ramifications of his theories that could be explained without understanding his extremely difficult mathematics: (1) If we could ever travel faster than the speed of light, we would be able to look back at the earth and see our own history; and (2) If we had a twin who remained on Earth while we traveled far away from Earth at 90 percent of the speed of light, when we returned to Earth, we would be much younger than our twin.

I asked my brother-in-law, Manny, to edit my paper discussing these concepts, and he did an excellent job. Again the teacher selected my paper and, to my astonishment, said this was an example of creative writing.

It was at this time I started to have trouble with math and French, I was failing these classes and not doing well in others because I was trying so hard in math particularly. In a meeting with the dean, he recommended that I take a semester off. He said that helps sometimes. I started again the next semester, and the harassment from my mother and brother Sidney intensified. "Why do you need so much time to do your homework?" "Why is it taking so long to finish college?" One day at suppertime, with other members of the family present, my mother became so critical that I tossed the plate with uneaten food that she had prepared against the wall and said I would never come back. I walked outside for a while and realized that I had no money and no ability to find a place to stay, so I came home, but I vowed to myself to make plans to leave permanently.

Before doing so, I spent the summer of 1950, believe it or not, on a cot in the physiology department at the University of Chicago, in the office of the country's leading expert on the study of sleep, Nathaniel Kleitman, PhD. I had a theory that snoring had a purpose. While still living with my parents in 1950, taking courses morning and night while working part time in the middle of the day, I would come home late while my parents were asleep. I slept in the living room next to their bedroom. As tired and sleepy as I could be, I had trouble falling asleep as they both snored loudly, and their door was open.

One night I actually listened to them snore. We lived a block away from an elevated subway stop on the Jerome Avenue, number 4 line. As the train approached, my father would snore louder and louder, and when the trained stopped, he stopped snoring. When the train started, he would snore very loudly, and as the train left the station, the volume of his snoring matched the fading sound of the departing train.

My mother would often come to bed after him, and, when asleep, she would try to snore as loudly on the inhale as my father, but when she could not reach his volume, she stopped competing and began to snore on the exhale. Because it sounded like one person snoring in and out, I listened to them several nights before I became convinced of the following:

The snoring sound we make—that we ourselves do not hear—blocks sounds that threaten our sleep. In my exchange of letters with Dr. Kleitman, he was very skeptical. He insisted that because snoring takes place in deep sleep, and we have no cognition in deep sleep, I was not correct. He did, however, invite me to spend the summer exploring whether snoring had a purpose. After listening to and taping couples in a residence for senior citizens and students in college dormitories, Dr. Kleitman acknowledged that I found some evidence for my theory, but said that I would need to find more to be convincing. I left with a feeling of failure.

Nevertheless, sixty-six years later, on a visit to my neurologist, Dr. Howard Maker, I was given a clue. He said that just as snoring occurs in deep sleep, so does dreaming. And he said that deep-sleep dreaming is a form of cognitive ability. Since then, through the Internet, I found that dreaming can occur in deep sleep, just like during light sleep, and the dream can disguise sounds, thus allowing sleep to continue. With further investigation, maybe it can be shown that snoring can block out unwanted sounds while in deep sleep as well as during dreams.

Wouldn't that be something! All loud snorers could unite. We would be able to declare that we have a purpose even when snoring. I plan to send my findings to a sleep journal.

An incident not related to why I was in Chicago took place on the day I arrived, and it was one I will never forget. As I was settling in for life in the physiology department, I was told a shocking story. After being introduced to Dr. Kleitman's assistant, whom I will call Steve, I was sitting alone with him.

He began bragging about being in a group that tarred and feathered "Negros." He told me of how he had tied black men to motorcycles and dragged them through the streets of Chicago. I was stunned and dumbfounded. There on the prestigious campus of the University of Chicago, and in the office of perhaps the world's most renowned scientist in the field of eye movement during sleep, Steve, a white man of about thirty, an engineer, highly skilled in wiring the brain for sleep observation, was not only a bigot but claimed to act it out with incomprehensible cruelty. He was so proud of his deeds that he could tell it to me, a newcomer, without a hint of shame.

As usual for me in those days, I didn't say a word, but he must have seen the shock on my face. I wondered, however, if he was telling me this to make sure I would not dare to challenge his closeness to Dr. Kleitman.

Moreover, it made me wonder about Chicago. I learned later that African Americans leaving the South in waves during the 1940s and 1950s often put up stakes in Chicago, and maybe his bigotry was part of a widespread backlash. I avoided him for the rest of the summer.

Moving away from my family took four steps: (1) In my last year of college, 1951, I spent one year at Army Hall, a City College residence for veterans. (2) In my first job after graduation, in 1952, I worked one year at Wiltwyck. (3) Then I worked six months at Irvington House, 1953 (4) I had forty-five years of marriage to Charlotte, from 1953 through 1998. Ever since, I have lived alone in my Mitchell-Lama Cooperative apartment. Contrary to my initial concerns, I have enjoyed living alone, especially as it has given me a chance to write.

Including my years with Charlotte, Chandy, and Michael, I have lived here on this out-of-the-way strip of Water Street, in a building whose back faces the East River. This building is around the corner from Cherry Street, where my parents lived in their first apartment in 1908. It is also on the same street that Felix Adler, founder of the New York Society for Ethical Culture (NYSEC), my spiritual home for the last fifteen years, worked to improve the tenement housing at the turn of the century. In short, I have lived in the same four-and-a-half room apartment since 1965—over fifty years—near to my actual and spiritual fathers.

It is a little surreal to wonder whether one of the tenement apartments that Felix Adler helped to improve was where my parents started their life together—which, to further the mysteriousness of it, happens to be around the corner from where I, the last living of my parents' five children, hope to spend the rest of my days on Earth. What is not surreal is that I have been active both uptown and downtown. On the Lower East Side with the L.E.S. Call for Justice and on the Upper West Side with the Ethical Culture Society. When possible I have found opportunities for uptown and downtown groups to work together with much success on issues of criminal justice.

It was in these parts of town, as well as Chelsea, East Harlem, South Brooklyn, Seattle, and the Bronx, where the ever-growing inner flame, ignited in a print shop when I was sixteen years old, lit the way to a checkered but rewarding life of thought, service, and activism.

Harold, Marsha and me, in 1944, Fayetteville, North Carolina.

Eight

"The Brightest Bulb of the Five"

Abraham "Abe" Markman
(1926 to Present)

Interracial marriages increased from 2% of married couples in 1970 to 7% in 2005 and 8.4% in 2010.

More than three in four Americans say they approve of marriages between blacks and whites. As recently as 1994, less than half of Americans approved. GALLUP NEWS SERVICE, 2014

In 2008 a man of color born of interracial parents was elected president of the United States, and in 2013 a white man in an interracial marriage with children was elected Mayor of New York City.

A. M.

❖ ❖ ❖

My nephew, Richard, my brother Milton's older son, mailed me a very nice card on my eighty-fifth birthday. Among the kind words was a quote from his mother, my sister-in-law, Gladys. She told him that I was the "brightest bulb of the five." My two brothers, two sisters, and I were the five.

My assessment was that of my four siblings, Sidney was the smartest; Esther, the most self-assured; Milton, the best personality; and Marsha, the best-looking and the most insecure. I was the youngest, and I certainly was not the smartest. Maybe what Gladys meant when she said I was the brightest bulb was that I had a lot of drive, and without a doubt, I lit up the place when I married Charlotte.

Before I go forward, however, let me say a few more words about my family. Our mother came from a peasant family in Poland and never learned to read or write, and she was very ashamed of that. After having Milton, Sidney, and Esther in four years, she found it hard to raise two more children. Marsha was born four years after Esther and five years before me. Marsha and I, especially, had an underappreciated, frustrated mother who was relentlessly disparaging and a warm, outgoing father who aggravated my mother again and again.

Milton was the firstborn, and he was my mother's favorite. On the other hand, he angered my father twice by going to Florida during the "busy season" of the family's costume jewelry business. Each time, however, he came back with a wife! Milton loved children; was funny, happy, and outgoing; and proved to be a great father and brother despite his negative references to my intelligence when I was a child.

I assume that Sidney, born one year after Milton, didn't have enough time to get the special treatment that the youngest usually gets, because Esther arrived three years later. I assume that as the first girl and the youngest, she received most of the attention. At the same time, Sidney, as the middle child, and much shorter and less handsome than Milton, must have needed to fight for attention.

Marsha told me several times that she felt she was unwanted. I was convinced that Mom's constant criticism of Marsha was the main cause of her being unsure of herself. My mother would make fun of her being skinny and compared her unfavorably to Esther. I was closest to Marsha, and sometimes

I found her leaning on me as if I was her older brother. Nevertheless, we both felt unwanted by our mother.

That feeling was confirmed when Margaret, an older cousin, told us that we were not wanted by our mother. We had come to that conclusion ourselves, but hearing it from a family member with a sense of authority caused us a great deal of pain.

We wondered how she knew that, what her motives were, and how many others in our huge clan knew this about us. Here is another example of how in the writing of one's life a second chance is opened to uncover mysteries of one's youth:

Margaret was the sister of Jennie Laefer, who, you might remember, was the first one in our clan, along with her husband, to invite Charlotte and me to their home after our marriage. The sibling rivalry between Jennie and Margaret was fierce. They both constantly spoke of and compared the brilliance of their children to the rest of the family. The pressure they put on their two girls to outperform each other had negative effects.

For example, Margaret's daughter, Barbara, at the age of about nine, complained of a severe illness. Though her doctor was not able to confirm her claim, she insisted that she could not go to school or function. We felt she was sending a message to her mother to ease up on using her as a competitive weapon against Jennie.

On the other hand, Jennie's daughter, Phyllis, seemed to be weathering the rivalry much better. All of us in my family held that view until Phyllis, then an adult, took me aside and explained in detail that her mother wrote the long poems she read to us years before, claiming that Phyllis wrote them.

Our clan was filled with instances of sibling rivalry among the elders, who then continued the contest through us, their children. As a result, the desire to show that you were better than your rival was so palpable that it became a principal determinative of many of our personalities. In my case, my mother fueled rivalries that I had with both my brother and a cousin. To this day, I have to consciously avoid such potential rivalries; otherwise I fall into them unwittingly.

Margaret, as indicated, wanted recognition as a very bright person of high status. My guess is that her revelation to Marsha and me was to remind us that she was part of the inner circle of the family who knew its secrets. When she spoke to us about it, she sounded like she was doing it in our best interest, and consciously, she may have thought so.

As indicated, I was hurt and angered by my brothers and my mother. Of course I was upset then, but now I think they were projecting onto me their own sense of frustration and failure: my mother's entrapment in "women's" duties and not learning to read and write and Sidney's not finishing college. As I have indicated, on the streets, I was also the youngest kid on the "Ward Avenue Window-Breakers," and my older friends often treated me unfairly.

As a result, I had a burning desire to prove my antagonists were wrong. I worked as hard as I could to learn and to do in life what I loved == working with people and joining them in a myriad of experiences in activism and service. I enlisted in or initiated campaigns to bring justice to the underdog and to the misunderstood. By doing so I was not only standing up for others but also for myself. I was striving for self-vindication. I was David who, I sometimes believed, brought Goliath an inch or so closer to his knees.

In my childhood years, my father was a great friend. Even though he didn't have formal schooling, he read a lot and explained so much of what he learned. He and others in the family were very interested in politics. Due to this, and spending so much time with my friends on the streets, I believe I gained a keen sense of what motivates people, not only in the political life of the country but in everyday life.

Besides the hurt feelings I had growing up, there were also times of joy, like when my father filled his Buick beyond capacity with family or clan on the way to the country and spending summers at the beach.

I wish, however, I could have another chance to get along better with my mother and my brother Sidney. I was happy to learn from Sidney's daughter,

Barbara, that Sidney was a loving father. I see evidence of that as Barbara and her family are close, independent, and caring.

In regard to my mother, if I did have another chance, I would complement her on how nurturing she was to her grandchildren, before they were old enough to make "smutzik" (dirt). I would be more understanding of how hard her life was. I would tell my father to ask for my mother's permission before bringing others to visit or live with us. And above all, I would be more patient in teaching her to read and write.

With Sidney, I would show more appreciation of how smart and artistic he was, and how we all appreciated the great contribution he made to the family business, and how good a father he was. (Because of his being in the service during the early years of his son's life and my moving away from the family before his daughter, Barbara, was born, I never had a chance to observe Sidney as a father.) I would try to understand the resentment he had towards me. I would try to imagine how hard it probably was for him seeing how much attention my father gave me while he had to quit college to help my father in the business during the Great Depression.

When Sidney learned that I was going to Chicago, he asked, "Why are you studying snoring instead of studying something important like cancer?" You can imagine how angry I was, but I should have asked him why he had to be so critical.

Even though it took me six years, I was determined to finish college. I became interested in the civil rights movement but wasn't too active in it. I became aware of my leadership abilities when I became president of the evening school's psychology club at the City College of New York.

I initiated a series on the causes of war and enlisted various heads of departments to give their views. Kenneth Clark, cofounder of the Northside Center for Child Development in Harlem, whose evidence before the US Supreme Court was most instrumental in overturning formal segregation in this country, was our club advisor. With his influence a more encompassing form of that series was adopted as an elective course in the daytime curriculum of the college.

Right after Chandy was born in 1956, I was accepted by NYU's two-year full-time graduate social work program. Charlotte and I decided that we wanted to take care of her ourselves, and Charlotte was willing to stay home with her. Our only income came from a work-study program arranged by NYU, my first year's fieldwork assignment at the Williamsburg YMHA, and from my parents. In all, we lived on fifty dollars a week. What saved us was that we were accepted into the Baruch Houses, a New York City housing project, on the Lower East Side. Believe it or not, our monthly rent for a four room apartment was twenty-eight dollars.

I worked ten hours a day and seldom arrived home before eleven o'clock at night. Charlotte changed Chandy's hours so she could be awake when I came home. We were so devoted to her care that we didn't leave her with a sitter for the first six months of her life.

In my second year in social work school, I was assigned to the Education Alliance on the Lower East Side, and my salary went up to sixty dollars a week — and the rent to forty dollars a month. In both years I was trained to work with children and youth in groups. I finished after two years, but I had difficulty because of my schedule and because I had continued to have trouble setting limits with testy teenagers.

After I received my social work degree, our life went very well for a few years. Chandy had a great time, as she was full of life and the center of attention from the older children in the project. The fact that she was practically white-skinned and they were brown and black seemed to have no effect on their acceptance of her.

Charlotte and I made many friends, so when we heard that a Democratic Reform Club was being formed, we joined with our neighbors. The Roosevelt Independent Democrats was started and organized by residents of a nearby union-sponsored and government-subsidized housing development for the middle and upper-middle class.

They put pressure on us to select, as our candidate for district leader, an experienced Democrat whom we didn't know. Charlotte, after deciding to go to the library to look up his background, learned that he had been affiliated with the Mafia. Nevertheless, the pressure to accept him grew.

My contingent was the largest in the club, and we vetoed their candidate. When we couldn't find anyone else, I decided to run. Although I won the support of the club, most members resigned. When I ran into the club's largest donor a week or so later, I asked him why he left. He said he couldn't support someone married to a black person.

One of the other members, whom I will call Dan, stayed and gave us good advice. He was Congressman William F. Ryan's campaign director. Ryan was the first Reform Democratic Congressman elected, and he represented the Upper West Side.

Dan said that if we keep the club open, we could force Mitch Bloom, the incumbent district leader, whom I was running against, and his army of building captains to stay in the district to campaign. In that way they wouldn't be able to help Carmine De Sapio defeat Ed Koch for district leader in Greenwich Village. It worked as predicted, and Koch did become district leader. One of my claims to fame was that I helped Koch launch his career in elective office—and without his awareness.

In my campaign, I was told that the captains went door to door, telling people that they shouldn't vote for me because I was married to a "shvartsa." It literally means black person, but it is as derogatory as the "N" word.

Once the election was over and we lost, as expected, we closed the club.

What could be a better measure of the "color of time" than comparing the photos below? Note the remarkable similarities between Mayor Bill De Blasio's family and mine and the vast difference in acceptance that we received by the public. The fact is that when I ran as a white man in an interracial marriage in 1959, it was a distinct handicap, but when Bill De Blasio ran with such a family in 2013, sixty years later, it was a distinct advantage.

Although my family photo was taken in 1973, I am convinced I would have faced the same wall of prejudice then as I did in 1959.

Chandy, Charlotte, Michael, and Me

Mayor Bill de Blasio and family on victory night, September 11, 2013.

Please notice the remarkable similarities in our two families: Both daughters were older and lighter-skinned than their brothers; both sons were brown-skinned with Afros; and both wives much shorter than the husbands. Even more interesting was that both light-skinned daughters had more difficulty growing up than their darker-skinned younger brothers.

In 1959, when Chandy was three years old, I made a mistake that had a negative effect on her and deeply upset Charlotte. I took a job working with pre-delinquent youth in Seattle, Washington.

Charlotte was very much against our moving to Seattle, but our friends and her relatives told her she should go along with her husband's wishes. Not only was Charlotte unhappy in Seattle and usually in tears, but our happy, outgoing little girl had a hard time being accepted by the children in the black, working-class neighborhood where we lived. Whereas her skin color did not interfere with her acceptance in the Baruch Houses, it did among her peers in that solidly black Seattle neighborhood.

One of Charlotte's dearest friends, who became my close friend as well, visited us in Seattle. She heard how unhappy Charlotte was and wanted to find out why. She took in the wondrous sights of the city, its flourishing and magnificent flora due to the constant rain, its beautiful lakes, and its glorious year-round snow covered mountains. She then asked Charlotte, "Are you crazy? This city is so, so beautiful. Do you want to go back to looking out of your window, watching some of the awful things going on in New York?"

Charlotte answered with great feeling in her voice. "That is exactly what I want!"

In the meantime, I began thinking about going back to satisfy my needs as well. I wasn't doing well with my assigned teenage group. Also, I was getting wet with Charlotte's tears indoors and with Seattle's rain outdoors.

After three months I promised Charlotte that we would return to New York in two years if she still didn't want to stay. Charlotte stopped crying.

Though we made wonderful friends, mostly through the Democratic Party, we did leave after two years.

Two full cars of friends accompanied us to the airport when we were leaving Seattle for New York. The same was true two years earlier when we left New York for Seattle.

Charlotte was always frightened of plane flight. After taking our seats, there was a delay, and we were told we could leave the plane until the problem was corrected. Charlotte refused to get off the plane with me and wait with our friends. Nothing would get her out of the seat that would take her back to New York.

The mistake I made in insisting on our going to Seattle was due to my patriarchal attitude. This continued to cause me trouble later in the marriage. Nevertheless, I made a good decision just before we left. I invited the teen group I worked with to meet Charlotte. The group of whites and Filipino Americans were very impressed that I had married a black woman. Until then their deeply imbedded prejudice against whites influenced them to treat me with disrespect, though there were important breakthroughs with two of the older members, one white and one Filipino.

When I was back in New York, I was invited to attend a forum on juvenile delinquency. A social work student whom I had supervised at the Atlantic Street Settlement was a panel participant. He had been appointed to their full-time staff. When he saw me enter the room, he stopped his talk and told the audience that the group I served proved to be the most responsible of all of the groups that participated in their predelinquency program. What he didn't say was how much they rejected my attempts to maintain discipline before they met Charlotte.

I believe that meeting with Charlotte caused them to see me in a new light and they were very impressed. Their disrespect toward me as an out-of-town white man turned to respect, and I believe they used their sense of guilt to show the remaining staff that they really did appreciate me and the settlement house program.

We chose to bring up our children on the Lower East Side, principally because of the diverse population. We were sad to learn that except for the time we lived in the low-rent housing project, there was considerable tension and conflict between the racial and ethnic groups. As a result, Charlotte, and Chandy in particular, faced a good deal of outright bigotry.

Another time that I caused Charlotte pain was when I worked at Union Settlement in East Harlem, and we lived in Gouverneur Gardens. It was because the community center I ran was open for youth until ten or eleven p.m. that I arrived home usually about eleven o'clock or midnight. Charlotte was having trouble dealing with Chandy, who as a teenager participated in the counterculture scene on the streets. Charlotte kept begging me to change my schedule so I could help her with Chandy. I thought Chandy was just fine, and Charlotte was being overly sensitive. I was able to accept Chandy's ways because I was working with teens who were doing some of the same things Chandy was doing with her peers.

For example, Charlotte was upset when Chandy grew a huge Afro. I thought this was a vestige of Charlotte's bourgeois attitude, which she thought she had eliminated from her consciousness when she left Atlanta. When I first saw the teens in East Harlem with Afros, I too had difficulty getting used to it. Nevertheless, by the time Chandy had one I not only accepted it, I felt very positive about it. To me, it symbolized the liberation that young people were feeling with the steady progress of the civil rights movement. To Charlotte, however, growing up with adults who were ashamed to be identified with anything associated with Africa influenced her more than she knew.

I realized too late, however, that I was making a very hurtful mistake by working so late. I finally became aware that Chandy did need help, support, and supervision. My allowing the difficulties between Charlotte and Chandy to persist during the fourteen years I worked in East Harlem severely damaged Charlotte's ability to establish a good relationship with Chandy. I came to believe that I was using my daughter to fight my battles with Charlotte.

On the other hand, a few years later when my son, Michael, was suffering from a bad case of asthma, I changed my schedule so I could return home by six p.m. That worked out quite well for Michael, Charlotte, and me. I started what I called a health schedule for him. In my readings I learned that in most instances, anxiety doesn't bring on asthma; rather, asthma brings on the feeling that you are breathing your last breadth.

One of the funniest stories during our marriage happened when the two of us took a vacation in Brazil. Our kids were old enough to take care of themselves, and Charlotte chose Brazil. She was fascinated by the fact that the African slaves found a way to maintain their culture even under Portuguese colonization and domination.

I knew some Spanish and bought a Portuguese language instructional tape. I heard that the Brazilians accept being spoken to in Spanish if you start the conversation in their language.

We were having a wonderful time seeing the sights and going to museums. We had two tour guides, and we were the only ones present with each one. One pointed out the favelas, or slums, and said we should avoid them, as they are seedbeds of drug wars and crime. Nevertheless, we wanted to visit them. We always wanted to see firsthand the poorest and most crime-ridden sections of any land we visited. So after we pleaded with the manager of our hotel in Rio, she arranged for a cab driver, Pedro, to take us to the favelas. He knew just what to do. He drove up to the church. A few teens were sitting on the steps. He called them over and said he would pay them to watch the taxi.

The church was built when the Pope visited. Its reverential beauty contrasted with the abject poverty, lack of plumbing, and dirt floor shacks of the surrounding favelas.

We walked through the narrow spaces between the shacks. People looked at us suspiciously. Finally, one woman agreed to talk with us. She was about sixty years old, gray-haired, and brown-skinned. She was quite handsome and had a proud demeanor. She showed us the inside of her shack. Other than dirt floors, it was clean and well-kept. She lived with her young adult grandson and her eight-year-old granddaughter. She was pleased to tell us that her grandson found a job driving a truck. I asked her if the girl attended school. She said no, because the school was too crowded. I knew the real reason. It was because the girls carried water quite a distance several times a day for their families.

Pedro enjoyed driving us around and introduced us to some of his friends. He said, "Ahvie, I am going to come to New York soon, and I want you to show me around." I told him that I would be happy to do so.

When we got back home, the New York Times had a lengthy article stating that the favelas of Brazil were the most dangerous, crime-ridden areas in the world.

A few weeks later, Pedro called. He said he was visiting his friends in Florida and wanted me to give him a tour of New York later in the week. I said I would be ready. The day before I was to meet him, he called and said, "Ahvie, I can't take New York. I walked around, and it is too wild for me. I am going back to Florida." So Pedro was comfortable in the most dangerous corner of the planet—but not in New York.

One of the reasons I chose to go to social work school was to gain insights into my attitudes and behavior. My growing self-awareness influenced my acceptance of the message of the women's rights movement. I examined and saw how I was hurting Charlotte with my patriarchal attitudes.

Therefore, I was surprised when she and Chandy were dismissive of the impact of the women's rights movement. Chandy thought the movement was advanced by white, middle- and upper-class professional women who had all the empowerment they needed. She believed their main aim was to change the subject from the real problem in society—bigotry toward African Americans.

My main effort was to try to keep growing. Now, I ask myself why achieving a satisfying level of maturity is still so hard to reach. My chief obstacle was — and is — setting limits. I eat too much and am distracted too often.

Another question that needs an explanation is why I have been so productive lately. Recently. Michael, my fifty-four-year-old son, said, "Dad, your eighties have been your best years." You may ask, "How come?" It is because I have eased up on trying to prove that I am special but only that I have achieved (and still am achieving) lifelong goals, like having articles published in a print magazine, *The Humanist.*

In a conversation recently with Michael, I told him that I have been handicapped all my life. Despite a profound drive to be innovative, creative, and accomplished, I carry the burden of only an average IQ. Michael then said, "But Dad, you are a highly intelligent person, and in some areas, you are a scholar. You have a good deal of other intelligences besides IQ."

I think that by developing my leadership, innovative, sociological, philosophical, and activist abilities, I give the impression that my IQ has improved mightily, but it hasn't. Even after teaching myself a rapid reading course, I still read at the pace of a snail.

In a <u>study</u> reported in *TIME* magazine in February 2015, which was first published in *Psychological Science,* researchers led by Angelina Sutin of Florida State University College indicated that on average, people maintain or increase their sense of well-being as they get older.

Despite my inability to achieve consistent mastery of limit-setting, and a number of physical ailments that are responding to exercise and doctors' care, I have never enjoyed my life more than I have than as an octogenarian and nonagenarian. A brief exception came when I realized I would be ninety in a few months, and my worry increased about the end of life. This was after always wishing to be older to make up for being the youngest at home and in the streets. My cardiologist relieved my anxiety when he said ninety was not ninety anymore. It is eighty or maybe even seventy. That seems an exaggeration, but it was reassuring.

Cassandra, Tariq, me, Mike, and Tiana

Nine

CHARLOTTE'S FATHER AND MOTHER

Horace Bruce Cochran, MD
(1893-1954)

Ruth Sewell Cochran
(On or near 1900-1982)

Charlotte's paternal grandmother was born into slavery. As a free married woman, she cleaned other people's floors and washed their clothes in order to earn enough money for her three sons' education. Two became physicians and the other an insurance agent.

In a black, upper-middle-class section of Atlanta, Horace Cochran became the neighborhood's family doctor. As mentioned he was a close friend of Martin Luther King Sr. and Benjamin Mays, the president of Morehouse College, which Martin attended. Mays lived with Charlotte's family for a number of years and was one of Martin's closest advisors.

In 1935, decades before Martin, Jr. became active in the civil rights movement, Horace led a boycott of an A&P supermarket. An African-American man was slapped in the face by a store clerk. Resentment toward treatment by the all-white staff in the store had been building for some time. Word spread to boycott the store, and large numbers of neighbors stood outside the store for days and refused to buy anything.

One day a group of men in white sheets came by. Horace told everyone to remain where they were outside the store. The white-sheeted group started walking away. Horace called upon some of his male neighbors to run after them and pull off their sheets. They did that, and the unfrocked men ran down the street and out of sight.

In Karen Ferguson's book *Black Politics in New Deal Atlanta* (p. 143), the November 1935 incident is described without basic variation from the story above that Charlotte told me and recorded, though it includes more details. Charlotte's father's name was not mentioned. For example, the community urged "black customers to stay out until [A&P] hired black clerks and assured better treatment of African-American customers. In retaliation, the company forced its black truck drivers and porters to buy in the store." The boycott continued for five years and ended in 1940 with the closing of the store.

Charlotte told me of other experiences that involved her father. He invited the Scottsboro Boys to their house. They had been accused of gang rape of a white woman in 1931. They underwent trial after trial for fifteen years before they were either exonerated or pardoned. Horace wanted them to know that they had a friend in him.

Also, each year at Christmas time, white young adults named Cochran visited their home in Atlanta. They talked about the slavery period during which whites and blacks named Cochran lived on the same plantation. These young men were very friendly and quite comfortable in acknowledging that they considered themselves cousins.

When I met my father-in-law, Doctor Cochran, I found him to be as warm, unpretentious, and as accepting of whites as Charlotte. Perhaps when he first heard of the marriage and wrote a letter of rejection, he thought that such a marriage would face tremendous hostility and that Charlotte and I would not be able to cope with it.

This was in sharp contrast to Charlotte's mother, who was cold, pretentious, and judgmental. She could have walked with her head high right out of E. Franklin Frazier's book, "*The Black Bourgeoisie.*" To understand Ruth Sewell Cochran, you would have to have met her formidable mother, Eula Sewell, Charlotte's grandmother. They all stood erect, dressed elegantly, and spent tremendous energy trying to prove that they were leagues above the ordinary stereotypical black person. Eula voted Republican. She said it was because Abe Lincoln was a Republican. It is likely, however, it was to proclaim her identity with the white elite of the GOP. Ruth was prejudiced against dark-skinned people, and Eula was thrilled that her great-granddaughter, Chandy, had less wiry hair than most blacks. She was a tyrant who drove one of Charlotte's favorite relatives, Uncle Bob, to leave home at fourteen. He survived on his own until he was old enough to join the merchant marines.

Ruth's sister, Ethel, like my own cousin Margaret and her young daughter, paraded her son John around to prove that he was a genius. For example, at the ripe old age of four, she had him read to us from the *Encyclopedia Britannica*. With constant pressure from his mother to prove by inference her own superior nature, John became so emotionally crippled that after she died, he ended up in a supervised home sponsored by public funds, unable to work or relate easily to others.

The person who made those arrangements was a devoted cousin, Nan, who made regular trips from Chicago to make sure John was cared for. We thought that Ethel would have wanted Nan to have ownership of her home when she died. We were surprised when Nan notified my son Michael that Ethel bequeathed her house to him.

Starting years before Ethel's death, she would tell me how she admired our children. It was as if to say she understood the damage she caused her own son. I was proud of Michael, who recognized the injustice of this and emphatically refused to take ownership of it.

So now it becomes clear why Charlotte left Atlanta and some of what motivated her to become a deeply committed activist on behalf of those treated unfairly. But there is more to tell. Returning to Charlotte's Uncle Bob, he too sent unmistakable signals that he was superior to most blacks. He raised black-spotted pit bulls for dog shows, and he was so very proud of his house in Long Island. He carried himself with dignity and was very accepting of our marriage. Although he had a long, common-law marriage to Florence, who was dark-skinned, he wanted me to find a lawyer who would write a will that would give title to his revered home and his expensive car to my children and not to his wife of many years.

I told him I would not do that, and my children would not want to take these possessions from their aunt Florence, whom they loved. She was loyal to him during the years when he spent months at a time at sea. Charlotte's mother and some of their relatives considered Florence not married to Bob and inferior to them.

All in all, however, Ruth did have some positive qualities. She became a librarian, was a steady presence for the family, and was a model for her other daughter, Helen, who also had a long career as a librarian (in a public school). Also, she helped make their home a place where the Rev. Martin Luther King Sr., Martin, Jr. and other members of their family were welcome.

The family endowed Charlotte with smarts, an education at which she thrived, a rare level of comfort with whites, an empathetic father who was a model for her work in civil rights, and a righteous anger that she channeled into hours of work with the homeless, the poorest among us, and many others entrapped in the chains of injustice.

Ten

CHARLOTTE ELAINE COCHRAN

My Wife, the Little Rebel
(1924 – 1997)

Ode to the Little Rebel*

Charlotte fit into a coffeepot at birth, was
MLK'S friend and confidante,
When at 16, and
Martin, at 12, already into philosophy,
Charlotte initiated and led a successful sit-in at College Park.
Straight A honor student from high school through college,
Exposed, and
Vehemently opposed,
Atlanta's black bourgeoisie,
With anger in her heart and little money,
Left Atlanta for New York,
Married a white man in the early 50s and against the odds,
Partnered with grit, joy, and cultural smarts to make it work,
Brought life of art to our son, and
Led parent takeover of daughter's on-strike school,
An anti-apartheid march, and
Among countless other humane acts,

The Color of Time

Stood on her feet for hours assisting the homeless,
Precipitating the illness that slowly weakened her life force.
Charlotte stoked the fire in my soul, and
The memory of the little brown-skinned rebel with
black and beautifully liberated gray hair,
Forever nourishes the flame of our unfinished love.
*Paraphrased from Appalachian folk song,
probably originating in Scotland,

—WIKIPEDIA

Charlotte said that at birth, she could fit into a coffeepot. When I married her, she weighed ninety-nine pounds and was five feet tall. Charlotte was quite precocious. She attended Spellman College High School, attended by the brightest female black students in Atlanta. In 1940 when she was sixteen and a senior, she decided to integrate the park near the school. It was called College Park and was surrounded in addition to her school by two black and one all-white college. Her fellow students were frightened, so Charlotte visited their parents and got their approval for their daughters to join her in a sit-in.

The students then followed Charlotte to the park, where they held their sit-in. The white college students tried to scare them away, but the black students held their ground. Charlotte then asked to see the president of the white only college. She convinced the president of the justice of her intentions, and thereafter the black students used the park with the whites. This occurred fifteen years before her friend was chosen to lead the Montgomery, Alabama, bus boycott.

Martin Luther King Jr. was four years younger than Charlotte. I asked her what he was doing while she was active. She said that King, while in school, was not an activist. He spent a lot of time studying philosophy. Before he married Coretta, he asked Charlotte what she thought of Coretta. I don't remember what she told him at the time, but she let me know that she did not like Coretta.

I have written of Charlotte's relationships with her parents. Her sister Helen identified with her mother and was very conservative. She said of Martin Luther King, who was attracting so many youth to the civil rights movement, that "Martin got his college degree, so he should let the youth get theirs without all this sitting-in and protesting."

Her mother and sister felt like many black people in Atlanta and in many parts of the South and even the North, who tried so hard to act "white." Because whites thought very little of blacks in those days, many blacks wanted the whites to think they were different and better than the rest of the blacks.

In defiance of her mother's wishes, Charlotte brought darker-skinned friends to the house. Charlotte was the first to tell me of cemeteries restricted to the "High Yella," or light brown-skinned, African-Americans. In short, the lighter-skinned "elites" didn't want to be buried with darker-skinned African Americans. I was amazed and wondered how widespread this attitude was. One citation I found was in an article by Robert L. Harris, "Charleston's Free Afro-American Elite." In this instance he depicts the elders of a church who thought that by restricting burial to lighter-skinned Afro-Americans, they would bring "a sense of social unity" among the light-brown-skinned flock.

Here, in brief, are a few of my experiences with Charlotte's sister, Helen, and her grandmother, Eula. Some years after Charlotte and I were married, Helen visited us in New York. She said she was ready to get married. We told her how happy we were for her and asked about her fiancé. She said she didn't have one yet but had decided on the details of her honeymoon. She would go on a cruise, and onboard would be a fountain pouring out champagne. We asked if she had discussed this with her parents. She said that her mother not only liked the idea but that she would accompany the newlyweds.

A few months later Helen called to say she was coming for a visit and wanted us to find a doctor for her to marry. When that didn't happen, she married a very light-skinned welfare worker, and her mother gave them a new car. We soon learned that he was an alcoholic who bragged constantly about his accomplishments. He died mysteriously within a few years.

When Chandy was five years old, her great-grandma, Eula Sewell, sent word that she wanted us to bring her to Philadelphia, Ethel's home. All I can remember about the visit was Eula combing Chandy's hair and singing this song:

Little Sally Walker sitting in a saucer,
Ride, Sally, ride!
Wipe your weeping eyes!
Turn to the east.
Turn to the west.
Turn to the one that you love the best.

Shake it to the east!
Shake it to the west!
Shake it to the east!
Shake it to the west!
Turn to the one that you love the best.

Origin may have been an ancient British marriage song, but according to the Smithsonian Institute it was sung to African-America children in many southern states for countless decades. It was as if her Grandma Sewell was telling Chandy and maybe the whole family that she was accepted for who she was.

As mentioned, Eula was enthralled with Chandy's hair. Though it wasn't straight, her hair was not as wiry as with most African Americans. Eula kept singing the song and gently stroking our little daughter's hair. Chandy seemed to enjoy the experience, and despite the odd feeling Charlotte and I shared, we were all taken with the warmth of the elderly matriarch communicating across generations with no more than a children's song and a comb.

Charlotte's father was not steeped in the bourgeois mentality and was a great role model for Charlotte. As indicated, Charlotte liberated herself from the culture of the Atlanta bourgeoisie and from her family and came to

New York as soon as she reached twenty-one. She proved to be much better prepared than I to deal with the various degrees of rejection we faced from our next of kin. It was her defiant stance that gave me the strength to stand up to my family.

Charlotte became a parent leader in the school strike of 1968 and one of the leaders in the local peace movement. She had the unique ability to just look skeptically at a person and bring him or her to tears. She could sense arrogance in a person at first sight. People throughout the Lower East Side, where we lived for many years, knew and respected Charlotte. One day I was asked to say a few words at the almost all-black Saint Augustine's Church about my activism. An African American woman, prominent in the church, who only heard about me because of Charlotte's volunteer work in the church and community, told me that until then, most people only knew of me as the man who married Charlotte.

Regarding our children, from Michael's early days, we realized he had a much different temperament than Chandy. Whereas she could hardly be contained in a playpen, Michael was content playing with his toys. When he was two weeks old, Charlotte declared that he would become an artist and live on the West Bank of the Seine in Paris. My macho reaction was, "No way, my son is not going to be an artist." But Charlotte was determined.

As indicated, she gave him arts and crafts materials, and he became fully engrossed with them. When he was four or five years old, on Macy's Thanksgiving Day Parade, we found paper replicas of the parade floats across the entire living-room floor. He was indeed influenced by Charlotte, but he was also self-directed.

I have written about Charlotte's difficulty with Chandy as a teenager and that I failed to help her. Our roles were reversed in dealing with Michael in his teen years. Charlotte would never admonish him. What infuriated me was that when I would let Michael know that I disapproved of his behavior, Charlotte would invariably contradict me by supporting Michael. I told Charlotte that she was undermining my authority as Michael's father, and I insisted that she stop, but she didn't stop.

One day I decided to leave her as a way to let her know how angry I was. When I packed a bag and was ready to leave, she got on the floor, grabbed my leg and begged me not to go. I went anyway and stayed at a Greenwich Village hotel.

I asked Michael to meet me at a restaurant near the hotel to assure him I was not angry with him and that he was not the reason I left. He was visibly upset but didn't say much.

Chandy was the go-between, and after ten days or so, I agreed to meet with Charlotte to see if she would change. Charlotte did not fully promise to change, but I came back anyway.

Another incident arose when I told Michael that I expected him to stop something he was doing. Charlotte again supported Michael. But this time Michael spoke up and said, "Mommy, you are doing the very thing that makes Daddy angry." From then on, when I wanted to set limits with Michael, I would take him aside, and he responded well.

Michael, now at age fifty-four, became a treasured advisor and helper with this book. After reading a draft, he commented on this part. He reminded me of what I knew implicitly but failed to bring to consciousness. In many ways I set firm limits on his behavior but hardly any on Chandy's. I realize now that both Charlotte and I were using our children to project our anger at each other. Whereas I was furious at her for undercutting my authority with Michael, she was so frustrated when I allowed Chandy, as a teenager, to hang out on the streets. I thought Chandy was strong enough to cope with her crowd. It was not until later that I became aware that some of her friends were drug users. The interwoven relationships of Charlotte and me and both of our children were, however, even more complex. For example, Charlotte had more influence on Michael's life goals, and I had more influence on Chandy's.

Charlotte's experience with our female neighbors in Gouverneur Gardens, the Mitchell-Lama Cooperative, was very tense. The women made her feel uncomfortable and unwelcome in the building. This went on for a few years until one day they realized how wrong they were. They actually started calling her the best Jewish wife in the building. They found out that though she was Christian, she would, during each Jewish holiday, cook Jewish meals particularly for me. With our kids and with friends joining us, these were joyous times.

Chandy arranged a twenty-fifth anniversary party for us and invited many of our friends. She said at the gathering that she was proud that we stayed together, as almost all the parents of her friends had split up. She said, "One reason for my parents' success was that they gave each other space."

In fact, we had our individual interests and supported each other in carrying them out. Charlotte, especially in times when we were short of funds, loved to wander the streets of the Lower East Side to find bargains and meet all kinds of people. She enjoyed telling me who she met, how she saved money at bargain stores or by finding small items in good condition left on the street, and especially how the old men flirted with her. That was sort of an inside joke. She would often tell me I could go out with Mrs. D. who was about eighty.

We each became active in groups and found ways to back each other up. Charlotte joined the Lower East Side Mobilization for Peace Action (LEMPA). In June 1982, as part of a worldwide protest against the nuclear arms race, LEMPA members participated in a march and rally in New York's Central Park. According to Wikipedia one million people attended what was considered the largest rally in US history. Charlotte, other LEMPA members, and I started marching from downtown New York to Central Park. I left the group about two miles from the park to meet someone who wanted to join the march after it began. I couldn't find him and proceeded to the rally on my own.

Believe it not, while I was taking a break on Fifth Avenue outside the park, I saw Charlotte, alone, walking toward me and smiling. She had a hunch she would find me and left the LEMPA marchers to look for me. We were amazed and pleased to see each other, joined the rally, and sat down and ate the lunch Charlotte brought with her from home. We couldn't get over meeting each other among a million people.

I worked with large numbers of teens and young adults often next to or in noisy recreation rooms. As a consequence, I sometimes needed to find a quiet place when I had a day off. I would go to a Staten Island park for reading and walking, or City Island for rowing. Charlotte would roast a chicken for me, and I would have a day of solitude and bliss.

Possibly as a way to return the favor, I let Charlotte pick the places we traveled to, and she had a reason for each trip: Mexico was to meet artists and enroll in a special sculpture class; Brazil in admiration of the African-Brazilians who still followed their cultural heritage during and since slavery by the Portuguese; Costa Rica for its University of Peace, its biodiversity record,

Madrid, Spain, mid-1980s

and lack of an army. Spain…I don't remember the reason, but we were greatly impressed; Paris, because she knew that if she got there she would never want to leave—and one day, sitting outside the magnificent Cathedral of Notre Dame, she repeated, "Oh, Abe, I would so like to live here forever"; and Montreal twice, because she was almost as comfortable there as she was in Paris.

There is no question that we had hurtful conflicts in our relationship, but we worked hard to resolve or mitigate them. Our marriage was very special to both of us. We had the adventure of our lives, had wonderful times together, and we loved and cared for each other. We were proud that we had a good marriage against all the odds.

Eleven

The School Strike of 1968

To building a lasting peace between teachers unions and communities of color, we can't forget their most painful battle of all.

By Dana Goldstein, Nation Magazine

Charlotte became a leader against apartheid in South Africa and, as mentioned, nuclear proliferation. It wasn't until the teachers' strike of 1968, however, that I had an up-close view of how she used her charisma and her smarts to rally people against social injustice.

We felt that Chandy should not be kept out of her junior high school on Henry Street on the Lower East Side of Manhattan because of a dispute between the Ocean-Hill/Brownsville, Brooklyn community and the union. Charlotte knew several of the parents—white, black, Latina, and Asian. They felt the same way about their children. On September 24, 1968, a few weeks after the strike began and in alliance with maverick teachers, we were determined to open the school.

Our broader mission was local control of the schools, and Charlotte became the leader of the women. By the time I joined their effort, the parents had indications from several teachers, some ministers, and a progressive district superintendent that they would cross the picket line with us.

Charlotte told me that many of the male parents and clergy were going to spend the night in an already opened nearby school. The idea was to arrive before the striking teachers the next morning, and I decided to join them.

One clergy member was entrusted with cutting pliers to open the school doors. In the morning, the clergyman opened the trunk of his car and gave us the tools but said he was not going in with us. District Superintendent Elliot Shapiro also declined, even though Chancellor of the Board of Education Bernard E. Donovan approved of parent/teacher groups keeping the schools open. Shapiro explained that he had to negotiate with the union in his district, not only about the strike but about other important matters, and he didn't want to be seen as taking sides. (Because he knew and trusted Charlotte and me, he gave the two of us a letter saying we could have complete access to the school.)

We had the tools and the letter, and we decided to go in. Two teachers were supposed to climb the fence, go inside, and cut open the chains on the doors for the rest of us. One very small, thin teacher climbed over the fence easily and waited anxiously for the other one. I was outside with two teachers and two parents. The other teacher who had volunteered to go in balked at the last minute because he was afraid that he might be dismissed and become eligible for the draft. At that time we were at war with Vietnam, and teachers were exempt from serving in the military.

I told them that I would go in. I was quite heavy, but the others hoisted me to a point where I could climb over the fence. We then opened the back door and let in several other men. We had to open the front door so the firemen could enter to see if we made everything safe before we let the children in.

One man who was not with us the night before, and whom we knew as a radical, took the cutting pliers, but his hands began to shake. I asked for the pliers and proceeded to cut the chains. When I opened the door, a *Daily News* photographer took a photo of me as I was letting in a triumphant group of parents. The next day the photo was on the front page. As you will see later, this photo (which I haven't been able to locate) had a remarkable influence on the young people I worked with at the same time in East Harlem.

Before the children could come into the building, we had to put on the lights and heat the building. The keys to the switch and thermostat boxes were in the custodian's office. People got hysterical. We were in a race against time. One woman came with an ax. Another parent had a lock gun. Still another tried to enter the room through a screen on the back window. We rejected using the ax, and the other methods didn't work.

In the meantime, the husband of the volunteer principal of the nearby school, where we spent the night, told me he knew what to do, and to follow him. He and I went to the basement, and he looked through many pairs of work pants until he found a full set of keys. He knew that custodians usually left a set of keys in their pants, and that is where he found them.

We were able to put on the lights and the heat just as the firemen arrived. The classes began and I was assigned to hall duty.

It was at that point that I saw Charlotte in action. She contacted other city agencies and was able to bring observers from the New York City Commission on Human Rights and other governmental entities. They were uniformly supportive. When the striking teachers refused to give the children enough room to enter the building, Charlotte contacted the commanding officer of the local police precinct. He came and instructed the strikers to move back.

In the meantime, we were observing the classes, and the children were getting the benefit of an excellent, progressive learning environment. We bonded with these teachers, and when the strike was over, we defended them when some were being considered for termination on what we thought were made-up charges.

After the strike Charlotte continued to assert her leadership. Her group selected a representative to be in the leadership of the parent-teacher association. We lost the vote for her because the striking teachers voted with those parents who supported the union's position. In response, Charlotte signaled for our group to walk out of the meeting.

Charlotte and the parents kept up the pressure on the principal. We had a lot of questions about his competency. When the children had difficulty with learning or discipline, he would blame the parents. At one parent/clergy meeting in his office, we raised the question of supervision of the children as they left school in the afternoon. We found that fights tended to happen at that time.

The principal refused to take responsibility, saying the teachers' contracts didn't require them to monitor the children after 3:00 p.m. One teacher in the room, Bernard Mechlowitz, spoke up and said he would stay after 3 PM and step in if any conflicts arose. He did and was very effective. Chandy and her fellow students kept complaining, however, about the principal. On the other hand, they reported on a series of thorny incidents that Mr. Mechlowitz helped resolve.

Charlotte took a contingent of the parents to see the district superintendent and complain about the principal. Within a few weeks the principal was replaced by Bernard Mechlowitz, who was promoted from his position as teacher to principal. By the way, Mr. Mechlowitz worked so well with us that he gained star recognition in the school system and rose to become interim chancellor of the board of education in 1989. As principal, Mechlowitz created a more open, friendly atmosphere in the school. He gave Chandy, at age fourteen, the space to lead her fellow students in a schoolwide teach-in on the Vietnam War.

Although community or local control of the schools didn't fare well citywide, the Lower East Side School District, under the leadership of a parent, Dolores Schaeffer, was well managed until it was forced to disband in 2003 when the state voted to institute mayoral control.

Twelve

OUR DAUGHTER

Chandelle "Chandy" Markman
1956–1981

When Chandy was three, we thought she was the best politician in the family. As mentioned, wherever she went on the grounds of the housing project, other children would surround or follow her. She was happy and radiant.

The situation for her changed when we moved to Seattle in 1959. We rented a home in an all-black, working-class neighborhood. Maybe it was because Chandy was almost white, or perhaps it was because she was a newcomer, but it soon became clear that the black children would not include her in their games. A white girl who was a few years older bonded with Chandy, and they spent a lot of time together. The girl, however, was intellectually limited, and so the quality of their play was dull and repetitious.

In New York, Chandy's drawings were quite imaginative, but when the two girls crayoned together, they both drew a girl with long, blond hair who always looked the same.

In the meantime, Charlotte found a wonderful friend through her participation with the women's group in the Democratic Party—Annie Outly. Annie had been a maid and cook for rich white people in Sugar Town, Texas, near Houston. She loved Charlotte, embraced Chandy, and "spoiled" me. She lived with her sister, and they both treated us like close relatives. We slept over many weekends, and they made special dishes for us, including the best gumbo I ever had. They didn't want us to leave Seattle, but when we told them we had made up our minds, they invited us to visit them when they planned to return to Houston in a few years.

A lot happened to Chandy in the intervening years, but before that I want to tell you the story of what happened on our way to visiting Annie in Sugar Town. Chandy was fifteen, and Michael was eight, and the year was 1971. Coming back from ten days in Mexico, we flew into the Houston airport. To our astonishment, border agents stopped us.

They said that the dogs smelled drugs in one of our suitcases, and they were going to open it. Chandy spoke up and said, "You are doing this because my parents are an interracial couple. This is a violation of our rights as American citizens."

I told Chandy, "Calm down. The men are only doing their job." I was calm as I knew why this was happening. Due to Michael's asthma, Charlotte wanted to take all of his medicines with us. Before packing to go to Mexico, I told Charlotte his new prescriptions had the same ingredient as the old ones, and Michael would need only one. Charlotte told me she didn't care and she packed five bottles of medicine that had the same drug, the purpose of which was to open the air sacs in Michael's lungs during an asthma attack.

The agents proceeded to go through every dirty sock in the suitcase they chose to open. During all this time, Chandy was furious. I told her that everything would be okay. The men then told us they didn't find anything and apologized. What really happened was that they opened the wrong suitcase. Michael's medicines were in another case.

Back in Mexico, Chandy showed her ability to relate to and stand up for people she saw as being mistreated. We stayed in a "pensión" (Spanish for guest house). It was owned by Puga, who taught Spanish at an institute in this historic city of San Miguel de Allende. Puga was an older woman who was a proud descendent of the Conquistadores. Chandy, who spoke Spanish, found out from Maria, who was one of the servants, that they were paid the equivalent of five dollars for six and a half days of work if they lived in the pensión, and seven dollars if they lived at home. For the live-ins, the half day off was to allow them to go to church.

Puga, in breaking in a new woman, Justina, who served the meals, would call her stupid if she didn't observe the traditional way of serving. For example, Puga expected that the guests would not collect and pass the dishes to Justina.

Later Chandy suggested, as a way to let Puga know that we objected to her treatment of Justina, that we collect the dishes for her. The next day when we did that, Puga said, "What you are doing is not our traditional way."

I told her, "What we are doing is our traditional way."

After that, Puga stopped calling Justina stupid, and to our surprise showed us renewed respect. Whereas previously she talked with pride about her background and the historical nature of San Miguel, she took us into her confidence and told us in detail about how corrupt the police in the town were.

A day before we were to leave, Puga asked to speak to me. She said that it was customary for guests to pay an extra 10 percent, which was given to the servants. Chandy checked with Maria, who told her that Puga did indeed give the servants the full 10 percent. Although we were on a strict budget, I was very proud of the family when we decided to severely cut our expenses and pay the full amount.

Before we left, Chandy asked Maria if she and her family could use more clothes. Maria said they needed them badly. When we got back to New York, Charlotte and Chandy organized two clothing donation parties for Maria, and Chandy continued to write to her.

Growing up on the Lower East Side brought Chandy much pain. She met prejudice, even bigotry, and rejection. It intensified at age five after we returned from Seattle.

The kindergarten teacher told her one of her drawings didn't make sense. If I remember it was our child's dip into the surrealistic. Charlotte and I both saw the teacher and told her that her remarks were completely inappropriate. Chandy didn't complain about that teacher after that.

By sixth grade she was accepted into an IGC (intellectually gifted class). Within two months she read twenty-five books, but her teacher wrote on her report card that she should have read forty books. I spoke to the teacher and told her that we were glad Chandy had read twenty=five books, and if she read any more, she wouldn't have time to have fun. The teacher said that the other parents, most of whom lived in an upper-middle-class cooperative, put tremendous pressure on the school to give the students what they thought was the best kind of education. I told the teacher that my wife and I were happy with our daughter's progress, and we didn't want her to believe she was not a good student when she really was. The teacher removed the negative wording from her report card.

In seventh grade one of her teachers made disparaging remarks about inter-racial marriages. Chandy spoke up and said her parents were in an interracial marriage and that the teacher was wrong to say what she did. The teacher berated Chandy. We spoke to the superintendent of the school district, but he said he couldn't remove the teacher. So we spoke to a lawyer. In the meantime, the teacher knocked on our door during the evening when I was at work and harassed Charlotte. Our lawyer arranged to bring the teacher to court.

Once in court, the judge accused me of previously coming to court with a false charge. I told him that was not true and that he would not be able to find any record of that, because it never happened.

The teacher revealed how disturbed she was by moving around the court and taking photos of Charlotte and me and even of the judge. The judge was obviously angry and set a date to hear the case in a few weeks. One of the biggest mistakes I ever made was offering to drop the case if the teacher would accept therapy. Her lawyer said she would never do that. I told the judge that I wanted to drop the case anyway. The judge admonished the teacher for her behavior in court and told her that she better not appear before him again.

In eighth grade, Chandy bonded with a Jewish boy. They seemed to have a crushes on each other. They were chosen for the two main roles in the school's performance of *Exodus*. When the boy's mother learned of their relationship, she forbade him from having anything to do with Chandy. Years later, when they were both in their twenties, he starred in a Broadway play that our family attended. Chandy stayed behind to meet him after the play. She joined us in a restaurant later and reported that he, too, was hurt when he was forced to break up with her. Sometime after that, he realized he was gay. Chandy thought he became gay because of his mother's intervention in their friendship. We questioned Chandy's theory, but we didn't say anything.

Returning to her preteen years, Chandy was on good terms with the white girls in our cooperative. One time she was even invited to a birthday party by a white girl. Chandy was the only one there who self-identified as African American, and when I came to pick her up, she seemed to be having a good time. When she was about eleven years old, however, one of the parents of one of the white girls she thought of as friends saw them having fun in the playground adjoining our building. The parent took her daughter's arm, pulled her away, and told her not to play with Chandy anymore.

In junior high she refused to stand up for the national anthem and was called into the principal's office and told that she had to stand for the nation's anthem. This time Charlotte and I went to the school and spoke to the principal. We told him that in a land of free speech, our daughter could stand or sit as she wished during the national anthem. He didn't bother her after that.

As previously mentioned, in junior high school, Chandy led her fellow students in organizing a schoolwide teach-in against the war in Vietnam. She showed a similar leadership pattern to Charlotte's. The other youngsters followed her, but she let them take the stage.

As a senior in high school, Chandy had high grades and wanted to go to Hunter College. The guidance counselor refused to make the referral, and Chandy asked me to intervene. I don't remember what I said, but the referral was made and Chandy was accepted at Hunter.

As a result of all this outright bigotry, Chandy became quite angry and also quite articulate in standing up for herself and for people of color. She tutored black children throughout the neighborhood, was respected and loved by her peers, and had a powerful influence on some. For example, a black teenage girl who lived in our building grew very close to Chandy. However, Chandy didn't like the girl's snobbish and conservative attitudes. Chandy, like Charlotte, would not tolerate arrogance and told the girl that she was not going to be her friend. The girl sulked for months. Finally she told Chandy she changed and wanted another chance. The girl not only changed, but after college she became an immigrant rights lawyer. She now teaches human rights at Georgetown University.

Another friend, a professor of psychology at Hostos College, recently told me, "Chandy had a powerful effect on my life, and she continues to evolve inside of me."

Chandy started to meet radical older people, and when she was just fifteen, she asked our permission to attend a political camp out of town. Charlotte questioned the wisdom of her going, but I approved. After that she started inviting some friends to the house, and I learned from listening to them that Chandy had become a communist. I spoke to her about this and told her how much I was opposed to the brand of communism practiced under Stalin. I told her that what I learned from my father was later confirmed by seeing documentaries and reading books about how millions of peasants were deliberately and systematically starved to death because they refused to join a collective. Chandy told me that her group, the Communist Worker's Party (CWP), did not approve of the USSR brand of communism either. Among other things, she said that the CWP was opposed to the USSR's imperialism.

Nevertheless, she felt that my brand of liberalism was too "wishy-washy" and that the people needed both clear principles to follow and the guidance of better-educated leaders. I told her that enduring progress can only come if the public is educated about the particular wrongs in society and then rise up in protest. I also told her that the public needs to become knowledgeable enough about relevant issues in order to sustain any gains made.

In her late teens, Chandy started to make serious mistakes. As a very light-skinned African-American, she over-identified with much darker-skinned people, and it affected her judgment. This became evident when she formed a close relationship with an older man whose skin color was truly black, whom she regarded as brilliant. When I met him, I was convinced he was far from brilliant. She was putting pressure on him to go to college even when he was not doing well in school. I told her he would be better off going to a vocational school. She said I was minimizing his abilities, just as her guidance counselors had minimized hers. At the age of twenty-one, she informed me that they had begun living together. My son Michael, on reading this chapter, said he understood why I saw Chandy as over-identifying with African-Americans darker than her. But when Michael had long talks with Chandy's boyfriend, he found him to be quite brilliant. Maybe I jumped to a conclusion while playing the role of the over-protective father. I trust Michael's judgment, but Chandy's newest boyfriend did get into trouble with the law, as did another of Chandy's boyfriends who was also dark-skinned.

The boyfriend she told me she admired the most, Carlton Brown, whom she met later at an upstate college, was the exception. He became and still is a highly respected school principal in a high expectation, middle-class, Long Island community and has remained a dear friend of the family to this day.

Chandy had always praised her female friends who had babies out of wedlock. She would often say that she wanted to have lots of babies. When I asked her how she planned to sustain a career as a human rights lawyer and still care for so many children as a single mother, she would say that she would manage.

One day she told me that she wanted to have a baby. I told her that I was totally against it. She equated my stance with the stance of my family in not accepting my marriage. I told her that having a baby before finishing college and before getting married would most likely cause her problems for the rest of her life. She would have a hard time finishing school, keeping a job, or finding a husband. Most important, she would be frustrated in not having enough time for the baby. When she continued to argue for her right to have a child, I told her that she would be completely on her own; I would not help her in any way.

She stopped talking to me about it, and I wondered whether she was pregnant when we spoke or whether she had an abortion after we spoke.

A few months later, she came to me and asked me to speak to her friend who had already had one child out of wedlock and was pregnant again. Chandy wanted me to try to convince her to not have the second child. I spoke to her friend, who listened attentively. Later I learned that she had chosen to have an abortion.

Chandy loved to write, and after college, at the age of twenty-three, she found a job as a journalist with the *Daily Challenge*. The following year she wrote for the *People's Voice*, a paper more aligned to her political views. Both were African-American newspapers in Brooklyn, where she lived. She was frustrated that people were not responding to the outrageous acts of brutality by the police against blacks. I said that this was her opportunity to educate the public by doing research and informing her readers of her findings. She started writing columns to do just that, but she didn't live long enough to witness results. She was twenty-five years old when she died.

To ameliorate some of the pain in losing her, I practiced the advice I had given her. I devoted the rest of my life to fulfilling what might have been her legacy: educating, initiating, and advocating social justice strategies.

Her death was caused by the devastating effects of systemic lupus on her body and mind. Systemic lupus is an autoimmune sickness. In November 1979, during a flare-up of her illness, her friends in the Communist Worker's Party held a "Kill the Klan" rally in Greensboro, North Carolina. I begged her not to join them. I told her how foolish it was to have a "Kill the Klan Rally" anywhere, and in North Carolina, it would be suicidal. I told her she needed to follow her treatment regime here in New York. As you might expect, the Klan became violent and killed five of Chandy's friends.

Later she told me that she went and felt compelled to do so because one of her friends had been shot in the back of the head at the rally while kneeling down with her arms outspread to protect the children in her kindergarten class.

Although my research could not confirm these details, one of five killed in what became known as the "Greensboro massacre was a female nurse and activist, Sandi Smith, shot in her forehead after bending around a corner." (Source: WikiLeaks.)

Cassandra, Tariq, Tiana, and Mike

Thirteen

OUR SON

Michael Bruce Markman
1963 to Present

To: Tariq and Tiana: *Written When Your Dad Was Just Born*

Recited at Union Settlement in 1963 at a talent show after I was hired as Program Director of the Youth Center

Reflections on Tomorrow

Tomorrow of no fixings in space
Tomorrow of heaven's shape
Tomorrow of marching fear
Tomorrow of soft, warm sending winds
Tomorrow of newborn colors
Tomorrow of visits to trammeled and untrammeled spheres.
Tomorrow that bursts in wondrous, inebriant joy
Tomorrow that struggles to be
Tomorrow that cannot be
Tomorrow that is everyone

Tomorrow that is each one
Tomorrow that we can all create.

*W*hen I read this poem to your Aunt Chandy, she was seven, and your dad *was a few days old. She and I were anxious to have him and your grandma home from the hospital. Aunt Chandy was especially looking forward to the next day, as it was Mother's Day, and the hospital staff allowed her to visit. It was also the time of the racial disturbance in Birmingham, Alabama. Chandy wanted to know what my poem meant. After I explained it, she wrote:*

Tomorrow is a rose
Tomorrow is a pretty day
Tomorrow is love for the family and relatives
Especially baby number 2
Tomorrow new people are coming into the world
And everyone is the same, colored people too
I would like to send this to the people
Who do not like you because you are colored
Tomorrow if they do not act better
I am going to ask President Kennedy to put them in jail.
Tomorrow I will be happy
Will you be happy too?

As I alluded to earlier, if Michael was not destined to be an artist, Charlotte felt that she was destined to make him one. She gave him pencils, paper, crayons, craft materials, clay, and paint. She took him to the Henry Street Settlement Art Cart and to children's art workshops at museums. Michael was fascinated with everything Charlotte gave him and enthusiastic about every place he went with her.

Having a bad case of asthma limited his ability to join his friends in outdoor play. That bothered him very much, but it did not stop him from keeping busy, working at his art for hours at a time. I would tell people that he put in a full day's work in his playpen.

Growing up on the Lower East Side was a decidedly different experience for Michael than it was for Chandy. In 1975, when Chandy was nineteen, Michael at twelve had not felt the full brunt of the backlash to the civil rights revolution. Racist views and practices had noticeably lessened in intensity and frequency. His life was challenging, but his world was much more accepting of him than it was of his sister.

This was the case despite the fact that Michael was distinctly darker-skinned than Chandy. Ironically, as a brown-skinned African American adult, he has had to put up with constant provocative stops by the police and other racial harassments.

The differences they faced in each phase of their lives affected their personalities and their activism. Chandy became a militant activist, ready to take on the world in her teens. Michael became a less militant but effective activist in his fifties as a teacher's union representative in the school in which he now teaches. Chandy's anger at the racism she faced came to a boil in the midst of the civil rights turmoil. His anger intensified when the advances of the human rights victories were being overturned due to the backlash against those victories.

Returning to his childhood, Michael did face some physical bullying by white kids. Also, his guidance counselor in junior high refused to recommend him for the High School of Music and Art, despite his unmistakable talent. After I spoke to her, Michael's application to the school was accepted, and he graduated four years later.

As a baby, Michael had severe asthma attacks. One day, when he was two or three, he had a temper tantrum, and I told Charlotte I was going to put him in his room until he calmed down. She said his doctor told her that doing that might bring on an asthma attack.

I told Charlotte, "That was his doctor, but I am his father," and I proceeded to put Michael in his room and closed but did not lock the door. I told him not to come out until he stopped screaming. He yelled, banged, and kicked the door but eventually stopped, and he came out. He never had a tantrum again.

I was determined to discipline Michael in this way after observing another boy with asthma who was allowed by his parents to have temper tantrums. This boy became overly demanding and acted as though he would have a tantrum if he wouldn't get what he wanted. I made up my mind that I was not going to let Michael become hard-wired with that kind of behavior. Michael's asthma attacks continued, and so I asked a nurse to help me figure out what to do. She said I would have to be a detective to try to find out what triggered the attacks.

Listening to her and learning from my mistake about not being home in the evenings to help Charlotte with Chandy, I told my supervisor at the Washington Houses Community Center in East Harlem that I needed to find a nine-to-five job. Thankfully, Alice Suzuki allowed me to do individual case work mornings and afternoons. Although I gave up my job as program director of the youth program that was open evenings, I continued supervising the staff that ran it.

To help Michael with his asthma I purchased an air purifier for his bedroom. In addition, I read traditional and non-traditional explanations of what causes asthma attacks. As mentioned, to tamp down his anxiety aroused in anticipation of attacks, I introduced him to what I called a health schedule. It included times to eat, watch TV, take his medicine, wash up or bathe, listen to my stories, and go to bed. I also let him know that if he was wheezing in the middle of the night I would bring him tea, which he knew was very helpful.

From my readings I learned that processed dairy and other foods might bring on bronchitis, and so we monitored what he ate carefully. In short, I was able to keep Michael from having attacks, except in the fall, when I returned to work after being on vacation for a full month. I then asked his pediatrician what I could do. He suggested we take him to the Allergy Clinic at Gouverneur Hospital in our neighborhood.

Michael was a very cooperative patient, and the nurses were amazed that he could look at a needle going into his arm without flinching. Also, in the middle of the night, when Charlotte would hear him wheezing and wake me,

I would tell him I was going to give him "Two five sips of tea." I thought this would be more calming and acceptable than telling him he must take ten sips. He would willingly take them, and his wheezing would stop or ease. One night when I tried to slip in a few more sips, he yelled out, "Daddy, that was more than two fives!"

When he was five years old, he suddenly complained of severe aches and pains in his joints. I took him to the emergency room of Beth Israel Hospital. The doctors took him into a room and asked him if Charlotte or I had beaten him. He told them that we had not.

Later a doctor said that through a procedure of eliminating alternatives, the medical staff believed Michael had a rare form of hemophilia, and there was no known cure for it. I had to go to work in East Harlem that night to open up the youth center. That was the most emotionally painful evening I have ever spent.

The next day, a hematologist told me the team of doctors wanted to change all of Michael's blood. What I had to do was get several people to come to the hospital as soon as possible and donate blood. I spoke to the junior high school teachers whom we bonded with during the school strike, and they all responded quickly and willingly. The massive transfusion worked, and Michael got better instantly.

When Michael was a preteen, Charlotte was concerned that Chandy, in her mid-teens, was imposing her will on him. One day we heard Chandy yelling at him. Charlotte wanted me to tell Chandy to stop. I said, "Let's wait a minute to see what happens." We then heard Michael raise his voice, and the yelling stopped. Charlotte never complained about this again. Thereafter, Michael was able to speak up for himself, and not only to Chandy.

At about age ten, Michael's asthma abated, and he was happy that he was able to go outside and play. At sixteen, he volunteered to assist the art teacher at the Henry Street Settlement, and two years later, he was accepted into the High School of Music and Art. Upon graduation, he attended the School of Visual Arts and received a four-year bachelor's degree, majoring in illustration. That was a prelude to a career as an artist and a teacher of art.

Soon after being hired to teach at the same junior high school that he and Chandy attended, Michael was considered an exceptional teacher. His supervisors wanted me to visit his class and see for myself how good he was, but I was not comfortable doing that. I thought my visit might distract the students. Nevertheless, in my volunteer work with teens in Lower East Side youth centers, I met several of his students. They first expressed surprise that I was his father. They then told me he was a terrific teacher. As further verification, his principal recommended him for a full scholarship for a principal-in-training program at one of the best teacher colleges. He refused, as he didn't want to be an administrator—he wanted to stay close to the students.

Lately Michael's artwork has blossomed. He had a book of illustrated children's stories published, illustrated other authors' children's books, sold many of his prints at Black Art Fairs, was contracted to illustrate an African American desk calendar, and curated some art shows. In 2015, he launched his self-published comic book, *Surviving the Storm*.

Though teaching full time cuts down on his time to create and promote his art, he would like to employ his most talented former students as assistants.

Although he was a talented rapper, he was very clear that that was not the kind of life he wanted for himself. He wanted a family and time to do his art. Nevertheless, there is one story about rapping that needs to be told. From the time he was fourteen, Michael wrote and performed raps. His friends called him "Magic." When he was in his twenties he met, a very talented and successful jazz musician from the Caribbean, Nass T. Hacket, the director of the "NASS-T BOYS ARMY." They collaborated on a long-playing record to promote Jesse Jackson's campaign for president. They received an engagement to play at a nightclub. Charlotte and I attended, but they were not allowed to perform till quite late. By the time they were setting up to go onstage, many of the guests were lining up at coat check to leave. When they heard Michael and the Nasty Boys, the guests returned to their seats. When Michael's sensational rapping and Nasty's beautiful musical accompaniment stopped, the applause was loud and long.

To their dismay, however, Jesse Jackson's staff was not interested in using the song in his campaign. Nasty spent five thousand dollars on the recording.

He gave all the unsold ones to me, and I still have them. The experience only confirmed Michael's resolve to concentrate on his family and his art.

In 1992, Michael married Cassandra Louise Carter. They have two children, Tariq and Tiana. They are excellent parents, despite the challenges of a young family. Living in Jersey City, they had to enroll their children in schools on the Lower East Side of Manhattan because that was where their babysitters lived. Over several years Charlotte and I and Cassandra's mother and aunt, residing within walking distance of each other, took turns caring for Tariq and Tiana. Juggling schedules and commuting made for constant pressure. Cassandra once told me she got up at 4:30 a.m. most mornings and worked nonstop at her pressure-filled job as legal secretary and in making a home for her family. Cassandra is indeed an excellent, organized, and hardworking person. Recently she was appointed supervisor in a well-known law office.

When the World Trade Towers were attacked, and when there was a transnational electrical blackout, and when the subways were not running, Cassandra left work early and walked from her mid-Manhattan office to the Lower East Side, about eight miles, to see if her children were safe. She did that even though I offered to get them.

Tariq, as a young child, would be funny and sarcastic so often that his teachers were happy to tell us that they enjoyed his talent for humor, and here's an example.

From the time he started climbing monkey bars, I'd climb up with him. At the age of eight, he asked his father, "How old is Grandpa?" Michael told him that I was seventy-five years young. A month or so later, when it was my turn to pick him up from school, he decided to stay and climb the schoolyard monkey bars. This time, while he was leaping from one bar to the next, I sat and watched him from a bench. Later, at his favorite pizza place, he leaned forward and stated with the fullness of his deep voice, "Grandpa, you are not seventy-five years young—you are seventy-five years old. While I was on the monkey bars, you just sat and watched."

Tariq yearned to be a teenager from an early age. One day, when he was nine and had been alone with me, he was quite mischievous. Later that night, on taking him to his grandma's house, I asked him, "Why were you acting so badly tonight?"

Without missing a beat, he asked me, "Grandpa, does that mean I am now a teenager?" Now, at the age of twenty-four, I asked Tariq if he remembered the funny things he said as a child. He laughed and said he thought of being a stand-up comic, but what he said as a child was not meant to be funny. He had no idea how to transform what he did into a comedy act.

The toughest test Cassandra and Michael had as parents had been when Tariq, at age fifteen, was diagnosed with epilepsy. It affected his sleep, his concentration in school, and his mood swings. Michael and Cassandra worked as a well-functioning team and found Tariq an excellent neurologist and psychologist. Tariq was put on medication, and his mood and schoolwork began to improve.

Unfortunately, when he entered high school and tried out for the basketball team, he was not accepted. Tariq was surprised, disappointed, and hurt. He overcame that feeling when he realized that he liked the Lower East Side more than Jersey City and that he no longer wanted to spend so much energy trying to make a team.

He had played basketball since his hands were big enough to hold a ball. He loved the game, played on teams that won tournaments, and garnered several trophies. While Michael had been restricted in the playing of sports because of his asthma, he had a deep desire for Tariq to succeed at basketball. He enrolled Tariq in tournament after tournament. As a result Tariq thought he had a chance to become a star professional player.

Although he was a very good point guard (the leader on the basketball court), I had my doubts. Tariq was very small, and though fast on his feet, he would have had to have been much faster to make up for his small stature. When I spoke to Michael about it, he said that he didn't want to discourage Tariq. One day, while I was alone with Tariq and Cassandra, I told him that it is very, very hard to be drafted into the professional league. He said he understood, but my words didn't carry much weight when he couldn't play for his high-school team.

Before this happened, Tariq had heard the story of the making of his father's rap record. He would ask me to play it over and over again. He was inspired by it. In an attempt to lift his spirits, I showed him newspaper articles indicating that other rappers were writing about their own illnesses. I suggested that he might enjoy rapping about how he dealt with his epilepsy. I found out later that he took my suggestion.

Nevertheless, I am so grateful about how well his epilepsy has been brought under control. For example, after a few years, the doctor took him off medication, and he has had no symptoms for nine years.

Besides epilepsy, Tariq has both attention deficit disorder and a learning disability that interferes with his comprehension in math. So after a year and a half of college, he took more than a year off.

I felt frustrated that I didn't have a good relationship with him. I spoke to him about my concern that he didn't let me in on what he was thinking. He said he knew. He shared that he did talk to a close friend he has known most of his life. Cassandra and Michael, however, continued to learn about his neurological condition and help him maintain a healthy self-image.

As he came to see me often to use my laptop and to look for job openings, I was able to set some limits with him that I thought he needed and it worked. From then on, when he promised to follow up on an agreement we made, he was very responsible.

After his twenty-first birthday, he took the initiative to reenroll in college, work out a plan with the registrar on how to proceed with the math requirement, and make all the arrangements for school aid. Also, he not only found a job in a clothing store, he was cited as "Employee of the Month" in sales. They offered him a promotion to supervisor, but he turned it down. It would have meant supervising others who had more seniority, and it would have been difficult to do well while attending college. He has been very responsible seeking better-paying jobs despite facing broken promises by prospective employers. He would just look for another job with special effort.

When I asked him how he felt about my writing about his epilepsy, he said, "It's okay, Grandpa. Epilepsy is who I am."

When he was twenty-two, I suggested that he, Michael, and I see the award winning film, *"Boyhood."* I explained it was about a boy who was different from us on the surface but faced many of the challenges we all faced. It worked out marvelously well as it started a series of the three of us meeting and being open with each other about self-identity and the role of hidden biases in our lives. What surprised me the most was that when Michael told Tariq that he and I were sometimes puzzled about him and shared our thinking in order to think of ways to boost his morale, Tariq looked like he understood.

Tariq Update: A year or so before completing all his courses at his community college, Tariq left the program. Nevertheless, to his credit, he has taken his mother's recommendation and is seeing a therapist. What is so characteristic of Tariq, and what we are so very proud of, is his determination to find jobs that would pay his way toward becoming a successful rap artist. Tariq is a talented writer and is helping Michael launch a new educational comic book. The story he wrote for it was sensitive and imaginative.

Tiana, at sixteen, is full of life and very capable of speaking up for herself. She is a very good student and an engaging conversationalist. I am able to speak to her with ease about profound questions of sociology and philosophy. Although she has a somewhat controlling manner, I found that she can be flexible. For example, in the years that I was one of her once-a-week babysitters, when playing games with her, she sometimes would tell me where to sit. I would just say I want to sit where I am. She readily agreed and moved her chair next to mine.

When I took her to the park, she would assign me to a role subservient to hers in some imaginary drama. One time, on the way to the park, I said to her, "Tiana, today I am going to be the superhero." She said, "Grandpa that is not fair." But she played the game my way that day, and after that, we would take turns being the hero who set the pace of our play.

At the age of sixteen, she endured a major scoliosis operation to fix the curvature of her spine. It succeeded beautifully, and now she is much taller.

Tiana Update: At eighteen, and with a quite good grade average, Tiana was offered scholarships and acceptance from three of the four colleges she applied to. She was, however, disappointed that only one school accepted her into its drama program. She decided then to major in psychology at Montclair State University in New Jersey and live on campus. At nineteen, after a very successful first year, Tiana is enthusiastically looking forward to becoming a sophomore.

Tariq and Tiana, — he almost white, and she brown-skinned — faced racism in ways similar to their Aunt Chandy and their father. Tariq dealt with harassment from the police as often as many dark-skinned youth. However, Tiana has reported very few racial incidents directed at her. Of course, gender and place count. Tariq spends most of his time on the Lower East Side and Tiana in Jersey City, which has become a more integrated and accepting environment.

Based on my experiences as a social worker, father, and grandfather, I have repeatedly observed that light-skinned children in inter-racial families tend to be treated much more harshly by the public. Looking back, I wish I had better prepared myself and my offspring to deal with this phenomenon.

Nevertheless, both Tariq and Tiana show determination and unusual flexibility for their age, and I couldn't be more proud of them.

Second Tariq Update: After learning how helpful he was to Michael on writing the narrative to another still-to-be-published educational comic book, I asked Tariq to help me with a chapter in this book. His comments were on target, and I changed it accordingly. Also, Tariq and I are looking forward to a new chapter in our relationship. He has decided to move in with me, after I let out the word that it might be good to have someone share my apartment with me at this time in my life.

Returning to Michael, from an early age he became steadily more independent. After I put pressure on him to find a summer job when he was fourteen years old, he eagerly sought and found jobs. He made up his mind within the next few years that he wanted to become an artist, whom he wanted to marry, where he wanted to live, when he wanted to get a car, how he was going to bring up his children in partnership with his wife, and when he wanted to buy a house.

The 1980s, during which time Michael became a teenager, showed how much things had changed in the seven years between Chandy's teen years and Michael's.

Whereas she was part of an era when her peers were advocating revolutionary change, Michael and Cassandra were part of an era when their peers wanted to live the American dream.

In my relationship with Michael, I have had to, like many other fathers, adjust to a reversal in roles. At age fifty-four, he calls and visits often, gives me advice, and makes sure neighbors have a key to my apartment and our phone numbers.

Despite his obligations at home, his teaching job, and his private artwork, we speak two or three times a week and have very long conversations about his children, my grandchildren, his new role as a union representative, politics, his art, my writing, marijuana legalization, race relations, and the Knicks. On some issues we go toe to toe. Recently, however, he said, "Pop, we differ, but you are authentic."

One time, he panicked when he couldn't contact me on my home or cell phone. He drove from far out in Jersey City, entered my apartment at 11:30 p.m., and shook me awake, while yelling into my ear for not answering either phone. It was then he spoke to my neighbors across the hall who were long-time friends of the family, got their phone number, and made sure they had keys to my apartment. He visits me often. We watch Knicks games and talk politics. How much more fortunate could I be?

Here's how: On my 90th birthday, he nonchalantly walked me into a large community room in my housing complex, where I was greeted by a throng of smiling faces. Family and many friends, many who had been my partners on the barricades of change greeted me. Carol Van Deuson, a former actress, and a beloved member of Ethical Culture ran the show with her usual fun and spirit. And Michael prepared and showed a wonderful video montage of my life.

Michael is a member of the teachers' union of Jersey City, New Jersey, called the NJEA, the New Jersey Education Association, and has become one of three union reps of the grammar school where he teaches art. He has assumed a leadership role and is proud of the advances they have made, just as I am proud of him.

I keep telling Michael that he has an ability with people that is his alone. He has a lot of Charlotte's and my outgoing personalities, but he has developed people skills beyond those he learned from us. He relates easily to people of diverse personalities and backgrounds, is an engaging conversationalist, and is upbeat.

UPDATE: Michael has received special recognition for his art and his teaching of art. In the autumn of 2016, he was asked to demonstrate his classroom skills on NJTV. In the video he showed the class the comic book he authored, Surviving the Storm, *about Hurricane Sandy and how our family prepared for and dealt with the storm.*

He asked his sixth-grade students to create a comic book page illustrating how they have or are surviving a personal challenge. One girl used her panels to describe how she dealt with a bully, and others described how they overcame family problems. The program was very well received, and Steve Adubato of NJTV invited Mike for a follow-up interview on his program, In the Classroom.

As an aside, Michael in his own comic book depicted Charlotte as being much wiser than I in preparing for the storm. After seeing him on TV with his students, I found a way to remind Michael of my influence in his life. My e-mail to him read, "You were Mommy's artist and my social worker." He got a kick out of that.

Mike accomplished much in the process: (1) He convinced a fellow Muslim teacher who was on TV with him to wear her hijab. After strong misgivings, she wore it and looked most comfortable in it, while eloquently introducing the project. (2) He was invited to be the commencement speaker at a graduating junior high school class in the Bronx; (3) Due to increased recognition, he is being invited to be a speaker at conferences on the teaching of art and how art projects stimulate better student outcomes in other learning areas.

Although he and I disagree on some political and philosophical issues, we have become as close as we were when he was a highly vulnerable child with asthma. He has now become a thoughtful mentor to me on my writing, and he orchestrated the most wonderful ninetieth birthday party that any father could wish for.

Wonderful news! In August, 2017 Michael received word that he was nominated for an EMMY for the video of his classroom teaching. He didn't win but I was so proud of him as was everyone who saw the video.

Fourteen

My Dearest Friend, Virginia Arnold

(1931 to Present)

Ginny hears and sees birds singing, dancing, prancing.
With ever changing images,
Cast upon canvas-like drapes,
Hanging augustly in the park,
Ginny paints the desert alive with cactus, quail, and
rabbits, with soft-colored hints of the unseen.
Ginny at seventy was a dear friend. At
eighty is my dearest friend,
My shield against the darkness,
With her quiet but eloquent wisdom,
She comes with affirmation, warmth, concern, and love.
With our dear friend Nina as a witness, I do
declare that I do love you Virginia Arnold!

—Recited by me on Virginia's eightieth birthday

I met Virginia sixteen years ago at The New York Society for Ethical Culture. After Charlotte died, I had the time to fulfill my twenty-year-long yearning to start writing about such things as universal child care and the public schools. I was concerned that in this country, with both parents working more frequently and the increase in single parenting, children were not getting the nurturing that my generation often received in abundance.

After a year or two, I felt the need to meet a woman. As indicated, I had wanted to join the Ethical Culture Society for decades and did in 2001.

I was very fortunate finding Virginia there. She has been a wonderful and dear friend. Many of the strengths she has do not come easily to me. Whereas I tend to be impulsive, she is a careful planner. Maybe the relationship works because she reminds me when I should be more disciplined, and I remind her when she needs to be less cautious.

Virginia is a fine artist with wonderful talents. As a new writer, she brings the keen and perceptive observational skills of an artist. She is also insightful and has helped me think through difficult personal situations. I constantly frustrate her because of the lack of care I give to my bachelor apartment. When I visit her, I am impressed not only with the beauty, imagery, and mastery in her paintings but also how intelligently she organizes her apartment's space.

Once in a while, Virginia blurts out her frustration with and at me. Usually, I think she is justified. Lately, however, I have found a way to tell her when I believe she is being overly judgmental. I don't argue with her when she is right, and she doesn't when I think I am right.

On September 20, 2014, her birthday, Virginia had a bad fall on her head. Her short-term memory was affected, and she was very anxious about it. I suggested that she just let her brain heal enough for her memory to come back, which it did.

After a few days in the hospital, Virginia stayed at my apartment for about a week. Because I remembered some of what I learned caring for Charlotte, I felt confident attending to Virginia.

I think our relationship works because we fulfill each other's needs. I am the activist/initiator; she is the steady, corrective hand on the helm. In discussing world events, Virginia tends to be pessimistic. Although I used to try to think of positive counterpoints, I have become more wary myself, especially of environmental matters. With our doubts about whether humans can outlast their self-destructive tendencies, we enjoy the quiet comfort of each other's company. Our activism is no longer in the forefront of our lives, but we still find a way to stir the pot of hope.

VIRGINIA UPDATE: In March 2016 Virginia was diagnosed with ovarian cancer but with a good chance to be with us for another five years or so. After the full force of it hit us, we tried to laugh and wondered who would outlast whom. Not so funny, but we tried. Virginia is handling this with remarkable physical, mental, and spiritual strength. And then the Great News: Based on the wonderful care and treatment she received by her doctor, the hospital, her niece Chris Cafaro, Carol Nadel Van Deusen, Dan Hanson, Monica Weiss, and Beth Everett and many others at Ethical Culture and to a lesser extent from me, Virginia was in remission! Unfortunately, after several months, the cancer returned, and her treatments have resumed.

As of this writing, there has been improvement again, and treatments have been suspended, at least for a while. We enjoy sitting in Central Park on our walkers, admiring the passing world.

Standing by Virginia's painting on exhibit, Creative Center

PART II
The Color of Grief

One

"Chandy Is Still Evolving Within Me"
Linda Anderson, her friend

Though the love for our children was profound and everlasting, we all knew that Michael was Charlotte's most precious person alive and that Chandy was mine. That was a determining factor in how Michael and I experienced our grief for Chandy and then for Charlotte.

When Chandy was age twenty-two, she was feeling quite ill and signed herself into the emergency room at the New York Medical College on Fifth Avenue. The assigned doctor prescribed a sulfa drug, which made her feel sicker. Charlotte and I were puzzled. After leaving the hospital, she saw an internist whom she liked and trusted. He referred her to a specialist who diagnosed her as having systemic lupus erythematosus (SLE, or lupus). When we learned that lupus was an auto-immune disease without a known cure, we were resolved to find out whatever we could.

Chandy wanted to sue the doctor for misdiagnosing her condition, thus delaying the real treatment she needed and causing her to suffer a negative reaction to the medicine he prescribed. But I convinced her to focus on her illness instead. We needed to find a doctor who treated lupus patients.

Charlotte, whose relationship with Chandy was strained, left her care in my hands, as did Michael, who was busy finishing high school. During the course of her illness, many of her organs came under siege. It attacked her brain, and she began to talk about whether life was worth living. Her body was so filled with steroids that it affected her digestive tract and left scars along her back. When her new doctor admitted her to Bellevue Hospital, she shared a ward with other very ill patients, and she became depressed. I convinced her to use her writing skills to write about the other patients in the ward. She did that, and it lifted her spirits for a while.

Chandy so impressed an intern that when she was transferred out of his unit to NYU Hospital nearby, he asked for a waiver on his assignments, and he continued to serve her. We also did several things to lift her spirits. When I learned that Bellevue did not send her records with her to NYU, I made such a fuss that not only were her records sent posthaste, but the NYU administration paid for a full-time nurse to care for her. Chandy enjoyed every minute of wonderful hands-on attention.

We called all of her friends to send her a get-well card and posted them on the walls of her hospital room, and that helped too. She pleaded with me to bring her pizza, but because of the high salt content, it had to be made in a special way. I begged and finally convinced a health food chef to prepare a pizza without salt. She didn't like it, so I gave it to the nurses. Later she asked for it, but I had to tell her I gave it away.

Our hopes soared when she was able to come home but she had to return to the hospital in a few days. In her last days, I would come and massage her legs. I asked her if that helped, and she said it did. A few days later, she asked, "What is the use of living?"

I said, "Life is so precious," and she asked, "For whom is it so precious?" Within days she went into a coma and never awoke.

I cried by myself until I couldn't cry anymore. After a pause I would start again. I went to the back of our building, and without anyone I knew watching, I pounded my fists into the wall. I knew the stages of grief: shock, indescribable emotional pain, anger, a profound feeling of guilt, and then anger directed at Chandy for leaving me. I allowed myself to go through all of these stages, and it helped.

Charlotte, however, was not able for emotional reasons to visit Chandy in the hospital. She blamed herself so much for their poor relationship that she was not up to it. It may have been her way to send a message to Chandy that she was profoundly sorry. But Chandy begged her to come, and she did visit.

After Chandy died Charlotte's face was covered with the agony of self-blame. She thought I held her responsible. I told her, "Charlotte, it is over."

Just hearing those few words so relieved her that she told me how grateful she was by asking me, "Abe, where did you get so much strength?" I think she meant the strength to deal with my grief while helping her overcome her tremendous sense of guilt intermixed with unexplainable grief.

What also helped was when Charlotte, Michael, and I sat around the kitchen table and told each other how much we enjoyed seeing Chandy in our dreams and believing in those few precious moments that she was still alive.

Charlotte said that Chandy told her that if we had a memorial for her, it should be a celebration of her life, and so we called her friends together. Charlotte took this with her old spirit and it was her path to healing.

A friend of Chandy's, an experienced documentary filmmaker and our neighbor, volunteered to direct the memorial. We soon saw, however, that he was intent on producing a well-designed program without our input. It would be professionally done but not specifically about our Chandy. Our family and friends decided to do it our way, and I was designated to tell him.

Privately in his office, I told him that we appreciated his kind offer but that we wanted to do the memorial based on our memories of Chandy growing up and becoming an adult who influenced so many of her friends in important ways.

He said that I was making a mistake because he felt he could use his expertise to honor Chandy as the special person she was. By then Charlotte was fully engaged. She contacted Countee Cullen's widow, Ida, and we held the celebration at the Countee Cullen Library, named after the brilliant writer of the Harlem Renaissance who flourished in 1920s.

We chose this library because the Schomberg Center for Research in Black Culture, where Chandy spent many hours reading and researching as a fledgling journalist, didn't allow memorials. It was truly a celebratory event. Ida Cullen gave the opening remarks. Some of Chandy's fellow poets read her poems and their own. Her revolutionary friends taught the children songs (which we selected). Our dear friend Phil converted her photos into slides.

Charlotte and I and her closest friends divided the narration of her life in synchrony with the slides from her birth to her death. Her memorial was very well received, and the head librarian decided to keep several copies of *Gap Tooth Girlfriends: An Anthology*, a softbound collection of poems that included three of Chandy's last poems written months before she died. Here is my favorite:

> Sing to me a love song
> Blue and mellow
> Lift the gray from over my shoulder
> Create for me the illusion of a mind at peace
> Erase for a moment the day to day challenge
> Place us high on a pedestal where we
> Might see the coming of the glory of thee—
> And watch through our four eyes the world turning/
> Spinning on an axis—
> Never yielding—never
> Yielding

Five years later, and after Charlotte died, the pain of losing Chandy was still so intense that I had to talk to someone. My friend Maggie invited me to her summer home in New Hampshire overlooking a huge lake that came ablaze each morning and evening by the sun. I spoke to Maggie for hours about my guilt, about working late, and not being there for her as she dealt with the streets of the 1960s; why I didn't listen to Charlotte, who begged me to change my hours so I could help her with Chandy. I was so convinced that Chandy was capable of handling herself that I was in denial of the difficulties she faced growing up. I must have talked for hours, and Maggie was a gracious and understanding listener.

From the time Chandy died, some of her black male friends, then in their twenties and now in their sixties, came up to me when they saw me walking through the nighttime streets of our neighborhood and told me that word had gone out that I would always be protected. Some of these fellows were drug dealers, but most were pretty solid citizens who knew how to cope with street life.

Michael constantly talks about Chandy's influence on him and his art. He gave his daughter, Tiana, Chandy's name as her middle name. When Chandy's old friends see Tiana, they say she is going to be just like Chandy. I told Tiana that people want her to be someone other than the person she is, and she smiled. Tiana is definitely a unique, self-confident nineteen-year-old living her own life.

Later I describe how Chandy and I influenced each other. She was on her way to accepting my advice about how to effect change. After she died I tried to put into practice the model of activism that I describe in this book. It is that progress is possible through many avenues but enduring change comes when people are armed with knowledge and a willingness to confront wrongs with nonviolent, civil disobedience.

Two

Charlotte, My Fellow Rebel of Forty-Five Years

One by one,
I grieved her
Diabetes,
Dementia,
Immobile legs,
Blindness,
Paranoia,
Inability to eat,
And so when her life
Slipped completely away,
I accepted her death without grief,
And from all that she revealed
Long before her death,
Charlotte gave up grieving long before I did.

One anecdote: After several laser eye operations at the Harkness Pavilion of Columbia-Presbyterian Hospital, and with her eyes showing no improvement, Charlotte told me she did not want any more treatments. She said she was willing to accept losing her sight because the treatments were very hard to take.

When she did lose her sight, she said, "I feel terrible that I am not able read to Tariq." (He was about three years old at the time.) I said, "I will find the books with the nursery rhymes that you know by heart, and as you recite them, I will turn the pages." That was not too satisfying. What did lift Charlotte's spirits was when I made the suggestion that I interview her on tape about her early life for her grandchildren. Her wonderful life force was reawakened with the recordings that we now treasure.

Several years before Charlotte's health began to deteriorate, we were lucky to have free legal service provided by District Council 37 of the AFL/CIO, my union when I worked for Union Settlement in East Harlem. It was then that Charlotte and I gave each other the end-of-life authority, making it very clear that we did not want to continue living if we were entering a vegetative state. If so, the well spouse was authorized to direct the medical staff to withhold life-sustaining measures.

During the time of Charlotte's continuing decline, I stayed home with her every day and night for four and half years, except for one night when her private home aide volunteered to stay with her so I could take a break. All of her doctors, whom I took her to on a regular basis, said how impressed they were with my devotion to her.

In the last two months of her life, we were assigned an overnight health aide through Medicaid. Charlotte stayed up all night and complained that her sole purpose in living with us was to have an affair with me. Her aide resigned. The replacement aide cared for Charlotte more and stayed despite being yelled at all night long.

I contacted a psychiatrist to evaluate Charlotte's paranoia and dementia. He strongly recommended that I take her to Beth Israel Hospital. He believed that the neurologists there were better equipped to more adequately diagnose Charlotte's mental condition. Before doing that I spoke to Michael about it, and he agreed. Shortly after being given a bed in the hospital, Charlotte's health began to decline. She contracted pneumonia, could not swallow food, and eventually lapsed into a virtual coma. Her hospital neurologist was definite in his diagnosis that Charlotte was virtually brain-dead.

Michael's profound love for his mother colored his insistence that the hospital continue Charlotte's intravenous feeding.

The medical ethicist arranged to see me alone and said that I had the authority, under Charlotte's proxy directive, to make the decision. I told the ethicist that I was about to lose my wife, and I didn't want to lose my son as well.

Within a day or two after that chat, and while still in close to a full coma, Charlotte died.

Years later, in 1997, I told Michael that I wanted to assign my medical proxy to him, but I wanted assurance that he would follow my end-of-life directives. He agreed.

Seventeen years later, in 2014, while driving me to his home in Jersey City, New Jersey, to celebrate Christmas with his wife, children, and other relatives, he confided in me how much he enjoyed decorating the Christmas tree with Charlotte year after year with the artistic flare with which they both were wondrously endowed and how much he still missed her.

I miss her very much. At critical points in our life together, one of us carried the other through extraordinary challenges. Although she is not beside me, what she taught me makes it easier for me to grieve my own slow motion and easily identifiable physical and mental decline, while I remain determined to enjoy life with all my being.

Seared into my soul are the precious memories of the little rebel, unafraid of the Goliaths in her path. Her strength sustained me when she was beside me, as it sustains me now.

PART III
The Color of Action

"Let the Circle be Unbroken"

FROM A SONG BY ADA R. HABERSHON

The first entry in this PART is about the Lower East Side Call for Justice. It is an example of a small circle of people able to make a significant impact advocating for social justice. We met in each other's apartments from 1992 to 2013. Other stories of my service and activism principally followed this model.

One

"The Lower East Side Call for Justice"

Presented September 2009
As a Platform Address at the New York Society for Ethical Culture

This year I will be talking about my seventeen years as chair and four years as treasurer of the Lower East Side Call for Justice (LESCFJ). I have three criminal justice stories to tell.

The title of the first story is: *Police, Alcohol, and Guns.*

It starts thirty years before the Call for Justice was formed. It was 1962 and I just started my job as program director of the Union Settlement, Washington Houses Community Center in East Harlem. During the first days on the job a Latino young adult was shot in the back and killed by a police officer. The community was outraged. He was running away from the officer after an altercation at a bar with that same officer. What actually provoked this shooting was a mystery.

I suggested that the community open a dialogue with the police. The idea fell flat. Within a short time, however, the staff of an East Harlem inter-agency counsel of center directors asked me to form a youth leadership-training group. The purpose was to start conversations with the police. Teens and young adults representing East Harlem settlement houses and community centers were chosen to participate. It was a very lively, bright, and articulate group.

We had a great time together. Someone invited us to have a weekend retreat with free reign of an unoccupied mansion in Manhasset, Long Island. It was so magnificent that it later became the home of a newly established International University of Peace. The Latino and black youngsters reveled in the multi-room estate. They marveled at the huge and attractive bathrooms, and all the ways designed to ring for servants. They had the most fun joking about a device in front of a living room chair. All you had to do was tap it with your foot and a butler would have been signaled to appear.

The group enjoyed a vibrant give and take about police issues. I remember one youngster saying how furious he was when the police in a so-called crime sweep on his block forced his mother to line up against the wall. I invited expert speakers on police abuse of authority and the group was ready to meet with the police and ask them questions. They were in a great mood.

Back in the city, we invited a police sergeant to one of our meetings. He personified a steel trap. In his mind, there was no arguing that the police were doing a great job. He kept to the worn-out proposition of the one bad apple in the barrel. He said, "Yes, in some precincts there may be an officer who should be dismissed and the department is doing what is necessary about that." He refused to consider any other possibility of dealing with police behavior. The teenagers and I were frustrated.

Before we could come up with another approach, Revlon Cosmetics made a presentation to the youth that they couldn't refuse. If they joined a group that Revlon was forming, they would be offered free concerts, ball games, makeovers, cosmetic and game kits. As the young people were leaders in their own centers, they would have found it difficult to leave their own widely separated sites two times a week, once for our meetings and once for the Revlon sessions. So when they chose the offer from Revlon, our sessions ended.

The altercation in the bar leading to the young man's death, however, continued to concern me. For three decades afterward, I read article after article about altercations in bars involving police shootings. Often it was hard to know who was responsible. In the following two *New York Times* articles, it was very clear who should have been held accountable:

"New York Police Officer Held in Beating in Racial Incident in a Bar in Long Island." White males came out of a bar and accosted a group of black youth. They started viciously beating one of them. When his friends tried to stop the beating, a NYC police officer took out his gun and told them to stay away. That allowed the beating to continue. As a result, the youth was severely injured, went into a coma, suffered damage to his vision, and needed extended hospitalization.

"4 Officers are Indicted in Beating of a Man." In a nightclub where the African American man worked, a group of officers who apparently were drinking heavily were quite boisterous. The man spoke to them about their noise. What he said to them was not indicated but they severely beat him later outside the club and chased him to a subway platform, where he fell over the side and was killed by a passing train. The officers were charged with beating him but not with his death.

As a lone citizen, I was frustrated as to what I could do. Then in 1992, some activists from the Lower East Side, known by my wife and me, asked if we would become charter members of a police watchdog group that they wanted to form. We knew them well as we worked with them in the antiapartheid and anti-Vietnam campaigns and during the 1968 school strike. We agreed to join this new effort and they accepted my suggestion that we name ourselves the Lower East Call for Justice. I was elected chair and I realized then that I could act on the police/alcohol issue. I was with a group that I could count on for support. I convinced the Call for Justice members to advocate for the following policy: *Police Officers should be prohibited from carrying their guns when they know they will be drinking heavily.*

I used our letterhead and wrote to Mayor Giuliani and to Police Commissioner Bratton. In response I received a letter from Deputy for Policy and Planning Michael J. Farrel. As indicated in the copy of his letter below, he wrote that the department's policy was, and I quote:

"…regulations state that officers should be unarmed at own discretion while off duty when engaged in any activity of a nature whereby it would be advisable NOT to carry a firearm. Such activities especially include those at which alcoholic beverages are consumed." That was not nearly good enough.

So I called Deputy Farrel. He said the New York State Legislature determined the policy. The law was that police officers are on duty 24/7 and must carry their guns at all times. I pointed out that sometimes after a shooting by the police in a bar, a police officer is killed for no apparent reason. It happened so frequently that it seemed to be a form of retaliation. He said he and other members of the department were quite concerned about that but said there was nothing they could do about it. It was up to the state legislature to change the law. I would have to contact Joseph Lentol, Chair of the Zoning Committee.

Why such a committee dealt with the police I never found out, but I knew that the police were rewarded special treatment by the state legislature compared to the treatment other New York City civil servants received.

So I did write to him. He replied supporting the present policy, and that "state legislation was not warranted." In short, he maintained that the policy as described in the letter below from Michael Farrel was reasonable.

Incidents of police shooting, killing civilians, killing each other, and even killing themselves continued unabated in and around places where liquor was served.

I then wrote to the Speaker of the Assembly, Sheldon Silver who was my district assemblyman and who I knew well. I sent letters to the editor and the Daily News printed one. I called into the Brian Lehrer and the Ron Kuby radio shows.

Maybe somebody was reading my letters to the editor or listening to my radio call-ins because things began to change. Clyde Haberman wrote a feature article in the *Times* about "The Dangers When Police Turn to Drink." He quoted Police Commissioner Howard Safir as acknowledging that police try to relieve stress by consuming alcohol. In October of 1998 a panel appointed by Safir recommended that "police should be prohibited from carrying their guns when they drink when not working."

Then a transforming incident occurred. I couldn't find a copy of the article but here is what I remember of it. During Giuliani's tenure as mayor he tended to give the police unqualified support no matter what they were accused of — here was one time he didn't.

An officer driving with his partner drove his police car into two bystanders, killing them and resulting also in the death of the officers. The driver was found to have a high alcohol level. For the first time Giuliani and Safir refused to attend a funeral for policemen despite intense criticism from the Police Benevolent Association. Then, finally, the police commissioner issued an order stating that *police officers who knew they would be drinking heavily off duty were prohibited from carrying their firearms.*

We won, but was it us or serendipity? Who knows? Although we felt great, and knew of no other group working on this issue, we didn't celebrate, but some of what we learned we were able to apply to other challenges that we addressed.

The title of my second story is "The Call for Justice in Full Bloom."

By reaching out to action oriented groups, the Lower East Side Call for Justice (LESCFJ) started to grow. Joining us and playing important roles was a young sociologist, Alex Vitale and a lawyer, Christian Covington. In addition, adherents of an international socialists group, old-time communists, Catholic Workers, and Reform Democrats either became members or helped us in campaigns. I maintained that to accomplish anything, liberals and those further to the left have to work together. Though at times there were strong differences, we tried hard to find ways to proceed. Most times the whole group supported an action; other times there was an agreement that only some in the group would go forward with a project.

Here is a compressed summary of our activities and accomplishments. We were very active in the campaign for a new Civilian Complaint Review Board (CCRB). However, we were very disappointed when the city council watered down the proposal that came from a strong city-wide coalition headed by Norman Siegel, former executive director of the New York Civil

POLICE DEPARTMENT

Office of Management
Analysis and Planning
1 Police Plaza Rm. 1403
New York, NY 10038

October 26, 1995

Mr. Abe Markman
675 Water St., Apt. #5C
New York, NY 10002

Dear Mr. Markman:

The Police Commissioner has asked me to respond to your letter concerning department regulations for off duty conduct of police officers. Your letter expressed concern about two areas of Police Department policy: police officers carrying their firearms while in bars, and officers performing any police duties while in or outside bars.

New York City Police Department policy specifically discourages police officers from carrying weapons in the circumstances described in your letter. The regulations of the Department state that officers should:

Be unarmed at own discretion while off duty when:

Engaged in any activity of a nature whereby it would be advisable NOT to carry a firearm. Such activities especially include those at which alcoholic beverages are consumed.

Many officers choose this option while off-duty. However, state law authorizes police officers to carry their firearms at all times while off-duty, and any change in this authorization would require action by the State Legislature.

I hope that this information addresses your concerns.

Sincerely,

Michael J. Farrell
Deputy Commissioner
Policy and Planning

Liberties Union. Nevertheless, after the CCRB was established and with the help of Sylvia Friedman, active in the Democratic Party Reform Movement (and a future assembly member), we recommended Earl S. Ward, an African American criminal defense lawyer and civil rights activist to be the Manhattan representative to its board of directors. He not only was appointed, he became its most effective member.

As expected, however, the CCRB proved to be quite weak. Nevertheless, while groups around the city were giving up on it, we used the CCRB complaint statistics per police precinct to take action.

When we met with commanding officers of our two local precincts, we insisted that they use COMPSTAT to discipline officers who had received multiple complaints. It was the same method that holds them responsible for reducing crime in their precincts. COMPSTAT is a computer statistics procedure to track crimes in each precinct.

Once a pattern of crime is identified, the commanding officer is given enhanced resources and personnel and is expected, in a reasonable amount of time, to markedly reduce, if not eliminate, the problem.

I wanted this method used to identify, track, and hold responsible individual officers accused of multiple complaints documented by the CCRB and given to us on request.

Results: In a three-month period, complaints were reduced to one in the Seventh Precinct and to zero in the in Ninth. Unbeknown to us we had duplicated the results found by the Vera Institute in two Bronx precincts. My thought of using the COMPSTAT was independent of the Vera Institute but we were thrilled to learn about their parallel study.

Lillian Lifflander, a charter member of the Call for Justice and an iconic fighter for justice in and far beyond our neighborhood, was a major contributor to our overall success. Ironically, however, even though she gathered the complaint statistics for us, she didn't believe in meeting with the police or in the results. She maintained that many who are mistreated by the police do not actually make a complaint.

Her decision not to join us and then throw cold water on our claims of success was rejected by those I did invite. Besides our members, a Catholic priest, a Protestant minister, the Henry Street Settlement CEO, a political party leader, a lawyer, and two sociologists took turns attending and praising our efforts. Nevertheless, we deeply respected Lillian and the strong objections she made.

At about that time, our lawyer/member Christian Covington became director of an interfaith group that intended to find out if the police academy was using the latest research described so brilliantly by Malcolm Gladwell in his book *Blink*. Gladwell pointed to studies that concluded that very often, police officers who thought their life was in danger became temporarily autistic. They were not able to read body language, and they often overreacted out of fear, using their guns when it was not necessary. He reported that if they were put into scenarios of virtual life-threatening situations over and over again, they could analyze better what they were actually facing and would use their guns much less often.

I wanted to join this inter-faith group. Christian referred me to its members. They said that I would have to represent a faith-based organization. By then I was a member of Ethical Culture, and I told them so. They said that Ben Bean represented the Ethical Culture Society. So, I asked Ben if I could take his place, and he agreed.

We were invited to the police academy and were told by officials that all the training methods would be revamped. They allowed us to witness one session using one of the new methods and one that had not been changed. In the new training, officers who had six or more complaints on their records had to attend a week of retraining. We were quite impressed with the session we saw of the revamped training. It was on helping officers to see how unethical it was to cover up for a fellow male officer who was sexually harassing or abusing a female officer.

We were quite upset, however, with the session at which the instructor used the old method. Newly recruited cadets were shown a video of officers dealing with drivers after their cars were stopped. It was an extremely authoritarian approach and lacked nuance. We were also disappointed in not receiving permission to attend the cadets' session on street scenarios about controlling their own fear in dangerous situations. Nevertheless, we had witnessed police academy training methods when organizations that were much more prestigious were turned down.

One day at a conference the LESCFJ members were attending, I saw a one page report of workshops for teens and young adults of color on how to react when stopped by the police. I was very interested and thought this was something I could do because of my social work training. We secured three New York City grants to print and update a manual on what to do when stopped by the police. Here is the cover page:

Artist: Rodney Black

When we conducted the workshops, we received very positive responses.

One director wrote to us describing how one of his young adults changed his conduct when stopped by the police. Here is a letter from the director of Kaplan House:

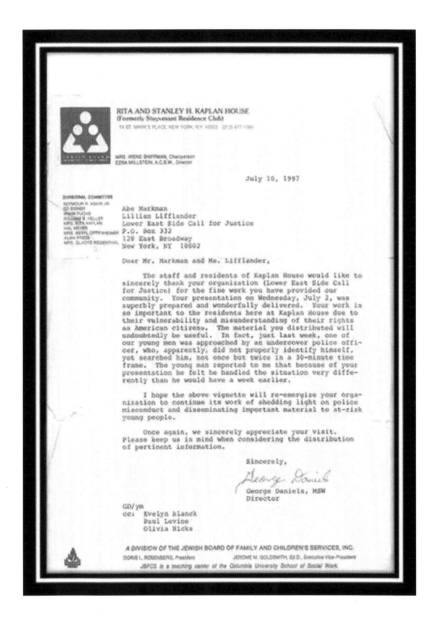

Over a seventeen-year period, we conducted more than 250 workshops, particularly but not exclusively with young people of color. It was a huge success.

When the manual was first published, I was invited to talk about it on the New York One cable news channel. Several organizations wanted copies. We were invited by directors of youth programs to return whenever their membership changed. We met in community centers, schools, churches, institutions, and alternatives to detention programs. Also, we held training-the-trainer and parent workshops. Our work became known to City Council Member Margarita Lopez, and she put through our last grant, even though we didn't ask her for it. It enabled us to give stipends to two college students who enacted police/youth street scenarios as peers to the participants during our workshops.

Our efforts were described in an article published in the *Villager*, a local newspaper written by a member of The Call for Justice, Bernard Connaughton, in 2009: "Getting teens to use their heads to save their lives." We firmly believe that if our methods were known to some of those innocent Black Americans killed by the police, they would be alive today.

We start by telling the young people that we are going to ask them a question at the end of our session that might be one of the most difficult they had ever been asked: "Will you cooperate when stopped by the police even if harassed, demeaned, or physically pushed around? Your life may depend on your answer. You can't win taking on the police by yourself." We tell them that police misconduct can be confronted, but only by organizing. We give them examples of how the huge, nonviolent rallies in the 1990s against police brutality changed community attitudes. When attitudes in communities changed, then attitudes of jury members changed. This resulted in juries convicting police officers much more often.

We tell them that if an officer comes toward you, make sure your hands are out of your pockets and at your sides. Don't just throw your hands up in the air, as that might falsely alarm the officer. If he or she asks you to stop hitting his or her car with your stickball, move your game out of range of the car.

The "cowboy shoot 'em up" mentality of the street crime unit, encouraged by the Giuliani administration, was principally at fault. We told workshop participants that resisting could provoke the police to harm you. There is much more that we cover. As indicated, one of the main techniques we use is police/teen scenarios in which we ask the teens how they would respond to confrontations and other situations.

Before we end, we again ask the question we asked at the beginning of the session and there is usually one person who says he or she would not put up with the police being nasty. We then would ask if anyone has a different response, and we do usually get positive responses that sound authentic. Most often we see the recalcitrant youth struggle for a while and then change his or her mind and agree to avoid confrontations when stopped.

It was one the most satisfying experiences for us to see participants, even some hardcore felons, change their attitudes right in front of our eyes and in front of the critical eyes of their peers. Also, we were happy to know that other organizations were conducting workshops with the same purpose in other parts of the city.

We worked in pairs. These workshops could not have achieved the success they did without the co-leadership of one white and one black enormously resourceful and effective women—Lillian Lifflander and Afiya Dawson. After over a hundred workshops that she co-led, Lillian insisted that we recruit a person of color as my partner and Afiya volunteered. As a former school guidance counselor and reverend in an activist African-American church, she used her wonderful communication skills to tell a personal story of how her son calmed her down when an officer was harassing her. Her son acted in her interest and to avoid having to intervene himself to protect her. She told other compelling stories as well, and the youth were especially attentive.

Sometimes, however, during a workshop, a substitute co-leader would want to take a hard line against policing as it is practiced in the United States. I had to convince them that their message might be a good topic for another time and situation, but it would not be helpful in reducing the dangers of face-to-face police/youth street encounters.

UPDATE: Lillian Lifflander died in 2016 at the age of ninety-six. Despite our sharp ideological differences, Lillian would constantly set up situations with hard work and then allow me to be in the in the spotlight to get the credit she deserved.

I call my last story "A Funny Thing Happened on the Way to Reform."
Members of the Call for Justice were active for years in the campaign
to reform the draconian New York State drug laws enacted under the gov-
ernorship of Nelson Rockefeller. In response to the "War against Drugs,"
Rockefeller signed the bill with a fifteen-years-to-life mandatory sentence for
drug dealing or possession.

We were fully involved in the two-decades-long Drop-the-Rock campaign, initiated and led by Bob Gangi, the former executive director of the
Correctional Association. It was intended to drastically reduce the penalties,
give judges discretion in sentencing, and provide more drug treatment services.
We also partnered with Elizabeth Fitzgerald of Justice Works (now defunct),
an advocacy organization for the rights of women prisoners.

At the beginning of the new century, in 2000, I met two members of
The New York Society for Ethical Culture, Barbara Levinson and Marcela
Montaruli, and Membership Director Ben Bean. We met at a New York
Correctional Association meeting and later on buses going to Albany rallies. I
was very impressed with their knowledge and commitment, and it was because
of them that I decided that it was time for me to join the Upper West Side
non-theistic, religious society.

Members of the LESCFJ and The New York Society for Ethical Culture,
NYSEC, often worked side by side in the struggle to eliminate the Rockefeller
Drug Laws and the death penalty. Besides attending these rallies, the members
of both organizations worked as a team at street fairs. Standing or sitting in
the hot sun for hours, we collected and sent about three hundred signatures
on petitions to legislators and governors, year after year.

Before tasting any sense of victory, we experienced a terrible tragedy.
Franz Lehman, while delivering petitions to Governor Pataki's office on Third
Avenue, was run over by a car. He was seriously injured and died a few days
later.

Three hundred people came to his memorial at the Saint Mark's Church
on Second Avenue. For some years after that, Franz's wife, who had not been
active with us before, joined us in Albany for meetings with the legislators. She
told the story of her husband's death and his dedication for reform. We always

made an extra visit to the office of our assemblyman, who was Speaker of the Assembly Sheldon Silver. Over time we saw his views change, and he became much more supportive of reform.

Alex Vitale, the sociologist whom I referred to earlier, became co-chair of the Call for Justice. Alex, by the way, gave a platform address at NYSEC after getting his PhD, becoming an associate professor at Brooklyn College, and he has written two books on police reform issues.

Back in 2002, and working out of Bob Gangi's conference room, he decided to devote his wonderful skills to the Drop-the-Rock campaign. Alex was charismatic, brilliant, and eloquent and knew many young, energetic activists. He attracted a formidable crew that included a Legal Aid lawyer, street performing artists, high-school rappers, and several other advocates.

We decided to have a two-phase civil disobedience campaign in front of Governor Pataki's Third Avenue office. In the first phase, after a rally across the street, some of us would put ourselves into position to get arrested. This would boost our chances that Rockefeller's granddaughter Mayla Rockefeller, State Senators David Patterson and Tom Duane, and others would volunteer to be arrested a week later. They were solidly behind the efforts to improve the way we treat the non-violent users of illegal drugs.

Several of us met a week beforehand to prepare for the first rally. The group wanted to confuse the police by not telling them in advance where we would be marching. We would surprise and challenge them to the point of causing an incident that would get publicity. I refused to go along and said, "Count me out." I said this action should not be aimed at the police. It was not a police matter. It was a matter for the governor and the legislature. The group disagreed, and I assumed they would go forward without me.

A few days later, Alex called me and said they accepted my position, and we would fully inform the police of our actions. And here is where the funny part begins.

Five of us showed up for the first round. I had a minor colon cancer operation about one week before, and I guess I didn't look like I was in the pink of health. An African American police sergeant said to me, "Why don't you get one of the younger people in the group to take your place?" Bob Gangi also asked me not to do this, but I said I wanted to go ahead with it.

We needed an ID with proof of residence before the police would arrest us. All I had was a senior discount Metro-Card. It had my photo, but without a home address, the police refused to accept it. Alex was desperate as he said we needed at least five people to get arrested to be able to recruit the better known people in the second round. He offered to drive me to my apartment and get proof of residence. The police were puzzled. Finally, they had an impromptu meeting with the Legal Aid lawyer, Alex, and Bob Gangi in the middle of the street without me. They made a dramatic decision. The police would call the MTA to get verification of my address. They got it, and we could proceed to get arrested.

The five of us marched across the street and sat down before Pataki's office building with signs. After a while the police came over to us and told us that they couldn't arrest us. We would have to move back and actually block the entrance to the building. And so we did. We were then handcuffed and arrested.

I was annoyed when a white policeman, while escorting me to the police van, grabbed my jacket and pulled me forward as if I weren't cooperating. I was tempted to ask him why he needed to do that, but I remembered what my message was to the youth who attended our workshops, and so I didn't say anything.

The following week proved to be a huge success. Eight people, including the dignitaries mentioned, came and were arrested. A feature column in the *New York Times* appeared in the Metro section, and articles in several other newspapers were published, and a report was aired on *New York One News*.

There were many stop-and-goes after that. Virginia Arnold and Nancy Ambruster of Ethical Culture came down to the Lower East Side to help gather signatures in blistering sun on the Sundays at several Memorial Day weekend street fairs, and Ben Bean and Marcela Montaruli and I continued to be active. In fact, Ben Bean was acknowledged at one of the Albany rallies in front of the three thousand activists who attended. He was praised for arranging a Drop-the-Rock forum at Ethical Culture in advance of this Advocacy Day in Albany and for his hours of volunteering at the Correctional Association office.

I think the members of the Call for Justice and Ethical Culture should be proud of the roles they played in:

- The dramatic reforms of the drug laws
- Drug courts set up all around the state
- Judges having more discretion in deciding whether those convicted might be sentenced to a drug treatment facility rather than prison
- Thousands of sentences retroactively reduced, resulting in the earlier release of some prisoners

In writing these stories, I realized that we often do not give ourselves enough credit for victories won. For example, my downtown group, the Lower East Side Call for Justice, and Ethical Culture were active players not only in achieving drug law reform. Some of us were also working side by side in the movement that led to the cessation of the death penalty in New York State.

And so I am continually amazed that a small group, seldom more than twelve people, could do so much and accomplish so much. I experienced that at Ethical Culture with the Public Issues Committee, and I experienced it with the Lower East Side Call for Justice.

Sitting in a circle, or around a table, or in someone's living room is where it all began. And it is where it all can begin again and again.

The main test I thought we passed was to be able to communicate with youth and with the police in a mutually beneficial way.

In brief: In twenty years, with ten consistently active members and meeting in our own apartments, we accomplished a great deal. There is a strong likelihood that largely due to our efforts: (1) altercations and killings at bars by the police and by civilians declined precipitously; (2) complaints against officers in two Lower East Side Precincts were practically eliminated over a three-month test period; (3) thousands of youth learned to avoid resisting arrest, while being informed that organization and nonviolent mass protests can result in better police behavior; and (4) working as junior partners, we witnessed the successful elimination of the death penalty in New York and dramatic reform in the Rockefeller Drug Laws.

After hearing those stories, a member of the New York Society for Ethical Culture, Alex Mogieleff, badgered the board of trustees to choose me for the 2010 Community Service Award.

UPDATE: Although we knew we held a much more progressive viewpoint than Sheldon Silver, we had no idea that he would be convicted of corruption in office; and in May 2016, one of the longest-serving and most powerful state legislators in Albany (and in the country) was sentenced to twelve years in prison plus huge financial penalties. As of this writing, his conviction was overturned, but he is facing a retrial.

Two

Looking Out My Fifth-Floor Window

Charlotte, Chandy, Michael and I moved into Gouverneur Gardens (GG), a Mitchell-Lama Cooperative, in August 1965. I waited sixteen years before becoming active in the affairs of this housing development, and here is what happened once I did.

A few months after my daughter Chandy's death in 1981, the family decided to take a week's vacation in upstate New York. We needed time alone as a family to share thoughts and feelings of our indescribably painful loss. We wondered whether we would ever be able to come to grips with the powerful emotions we were experiencing.

On coming home we found a distraction. We learned that the residents of our building were quite upset. The site manager, whom I will call J. P., had rented out our common storage room to a numbers dealer.

GG is located in the borough of Manhattan, New York City, and in its six, twenty-one story buildings, there are 784 apartments. It is subsidized and supervised by city, state, and federal housing agencies, under the state initiated Mitchell-Lama program. The original goal was to discourage middle-class families from leaving the city by providing affordable, limited equity housing. Its buildings lie adjacent to the Vladeck Houses, a low-rent city project. The hope of the designers was that a neighborhood bonding would take place

140

between the residents of both developments, and this has happened from time to time.

A day or two after our return from upstate, the residents' anger remained as Michael and I heard noise from the street. We looked out of our fifth-floor living room window and saw a large group of neighbors listening to someone. I recognized the person speaking as M. R., who lived in our building. He said he was representing J. P., the site manager, and offered to form a committee to deal with the "numbers" problem.

I told Michael I wouldn't allow M. R. to manipulate this situation as he had in other disputes in the wider community. Charlotte and I were familiar with his confidence game "hustles."

Upon joining the gathering I said what we needed was to elect someone from our building who could alert us to objectionable actions by the board. People liked the idea and were willing to meet in our lobby in a few days. M. R. thanked me for doing his job, although I suspected J. P. had offered him money to try to defuse our anger.

My fellow cooperators were very supportive of my leadership, and residents of all six buildings offered to help. I realized that I could keep Chandy's spirit alive within me by becoming involved in my own community.

What follows is an outline of a twenty-four-year story of how I tried to fulfill the path she began in a promising way before her death. I was not going to try, however, to fulfill her radical agenda, but rather her short-lived process of learning, educating, and leading in the struggle for a progressive change. It was a process, as indicated, that I encouraged her to adopt as a newly hired activist/journalist, and it is the process I have used myself ever since.

We began to suspect that we were dealing with an authoritarian board and site manager giving off questionable signals when:

- A large number of new improvements were announced and begun without informing us of how they would be funded. When I asked at a community meeting how they were being paid for, J. P. said that he was funding them himself. His answer seemed intended to cut off discussion of the issue.

- We created a logo for our leaflets and called for a co-op-wide meeting to air our questions. After we distributed them throughout the six buildings, someone copied our logo and distributed a flyer announcing the cancellation of the meeting.
- One of our friends asked for a petition to run for the board and was forcibly escorted by J. P. out of the management office.
- I received a phone call from a board member who let me know how disappointed she was in me. She wanted to know why I wanted to hold meetings opposing the board, as the trustees were working in everyone's interest.
- When I kept holding meetings and gaining support by explaining what was happening, someone shot BB pellets through our windows. Shortly afterward a fire occurred in our elevator.
- The board changed the bylaws to keep some directors in office beyond their terms. In addition, in order to win elections, they used deceptive, dishonest, and inflammatory tactics.
- At a GG election for the board, J. P. had guard dogs on a leash patrolling the hallways. We were astonished (but hardly intimidated), and we decided to hire a lawyer in preparation for involving the public housing departments.
- When our lawyer arrived on our grounds, J. P. took him by the arm and told him to get off *his* property.

Through a series of information flyers, I kept the cooperators informed, and our support continued to grow. We called a meeting at the local public school, and about five hundred residents attended. During the meeting, Board President L. C. marched down the aisle, came onstage where I was speaking, and handed me a subpoena. I continued the meeting without stopping to read it. After the planned agenda was completed, I was asked to read it. Instead I handed it to our lawyer, who said it had no merit and succeeded in having it dismissed.

The board removed the present management company and hired J. P. to be the new management agent. When we discovered that the board changed the bylaws to keep some directors beyond their terms of office, we applied for and received a subpoena against the board and J. P.

With a few of our committee members accompanying me, we found a police officer to stand beside me while I delivered the subpoena. I knocked on J. P.'s office door and identified myself. When he opened, I handed him the summons. L. C.'s brother, who was also on the board, came out of the office and banged his fist against the wall, shouting, "This will not stand."

During that time, I was elected chair of our co-op association. It was called the Six Buildings House Committee (6BHC), and I looked for cooperators who could help. Joining us was a lawyer, an executive of a nonprofit affordable housing agency, an engineer, an economist, a community activist, a brilliant businessman, and other competent and ethical people. Interestingly, four of our most active members were in interracial or interethnic marriages.

To get help, we visited all the governmental authorities: the New York State Attorney General and representatives of federal, state, and city housing departments that had responsibility for overseeing aspects of GG's operations. They all took the position that they didn't want to get involved in a board/ resident dispute.

Someone suggested that Miriam Friedlander, our city council member, might help. We weren't sure, as she was considered a radical with a confrontational manner, and other council members found her difficult to work with.

Nevertheless, she proved to be our hero. After we presented our case to her, she said she believed us and called a meeting of the representatives of all the housing agencies involved in supervising our development. At that meeting she insisted that someone in the room must take action against this runaway board.

During the meeting, we were turned down by federal and state housing officials. But Ruth Lerner, the deputy commissioner of Housing, Development, and Preservation (HPD of NYC), said she would hold a hearing to determine the truth about the situation. She made that statement despite a plea from her lawyer that could be heard in every corner of the room not to get involved.

At the hearing, she listened to us and the lawyers from both sides, and she said she would recommend that the city dismiss the board and assign HPD to administer Gouverneur Gardens. On the way out, I told her that we would inform her when we thought we would be ready to hold a new election for the board.

We were in a mood to celebrate when, around three p.m. the next day, I received a phone call from Miriam Friedlander. She said that the HPD commissioner, Ruth Lerner's boss, wanted us to have a petition on his desk the following morning with a significant proportion of signatures of shareholders who were in favor of the city taking control of GG.

I wrote a petition and called members of our co-op association, and by nine thirty that evening, we had obtained 300 shareholder signatures out of the 784 who were eligible to sign. Within days, Bernard Gurrin, an HPD employee who owned a private real estate company, was assigned to run our development. The L. C. and J. P. era was finally over, and J. P. wanted us to know how angry he was with us. One late night, soon after Gurrin's appointment, I was walking alongside GG's buildings and heard J. P.'s voice calling me. He had stopped his car in the middle of the street with L. C., who was now the ex-board president, sitting at his side. He called out in an emphatic voice, "Markman, come over here. I want to talk to you." I just kept walking. That was not the first time he tried to intimidate me, but it was the last.

Bernard Gurrin asked me to recommend cooperators for a GG advisory council that he would lead. I insisted on people who had expertise and/or ability to dialogue. A few who were active with us were quite upset when I didn't choose them. I found them self-absorbed, but I could have been more tactful.

After a year of good governance by the advisory council and the new management, we told Mr. Gurrin we were ready for an election. We insisted that we would only support candidates who would not vote to go private. Going private was popular among some residents as it would mean our being able to sell our desirable apartments for hundreds of thousands of dollars. We obtained our apartments for only $600 a room.

We felt that the Mitchel-Lama program was there for us when we needed it, and we wanted to make it available to others in need.

While remaining chair of 6BHC, I ran for vice-president, and Sigmund Israel, a Legal Aid Society lawyer, ran for president. We recruited ten other well-qualified candidates, and our entire slate was elected.

Bernard Gurrin had his own management company, and despite the questionable relationship he had as a former employee of HPD, we were impressed with him and his firm's operations and worked out a contract with him to manage our development. He and his son suggested new vendors for security and the laundry machines and introduced us to financiers who argued for going private. We were skeptical of Gurrin's motivation. We wondered if and how his company would benefit from such moves.

At my initiation, Sig Israel and I met with Gurrin in his office and told him that we didn't want to change vendors, and we were not interested in having the project go private. After that the Gurrin father-and-son team never suggested a vendor replacement unless we asked for help in finding one.

For most of our twenty-four-year tenure, or from 1981 to 2005, we kept monthly maintenance fees below $600 for a two-bedroom apartment. We hired a housing consultant who outlined a five-year upgrade, features of which included elevator repairs and replacement of all windows.

- Before becoming active, I had observed that over the previous sixteen years of GG's governance, we had thirty-two site managers. I concluded that residents overwhelmed the managers with complaints and requests for special treatment, which caused them to leave. Therefore, I proposed the following:
  1. A resident with a complaint should take it to the site manager.
  2. If not satisfied an appeal could be made to the appropriate committee.
  3. Every committee should be chaired by a board member.
  4. If the issue is still unresolved, it could be taken to the full board.

This system worked exceedingly well for about ten years. Residents accepted the process, complaints were generally resolved, and there were only two site manager changes. That stood until someone who was opposed to us was elected for the first time. L.N., the victor, said that no one would stop him from putting pressure on the site manager if a neighbor needed help. He would take the issue directly to the board if necessary. He would thereby bypass the committee's mediation and resolution responsibilities. He did that and succeeded in weakening our system.

In and around Building 6, where I lived, we faced two formidable crime problems. I won't go into details to protect those of us who worked silently and effectively as a team despite the extreme danger. But I will say that I and the neighbors who trusted me succeeded in not only ridding both operations from our building and from across the street, we succeeded in completely closing them down from operating anywhere. We accomplished this despite the reluctance of the police to act. I was very proud of myself as I was the most vulnerable and the one who found a way to use the necessary leverages and resources as a board member in a timely and appropriate manner. This was among the many times Charlotte was sympathetic but concerned about our family and thought I was crazy for taking such chances.

While continuing to achieve noteworthy gains, we faced a fierce and growing opposition. Despite the fact that we (1) forced Mayor Koch's administration to remove two jail barges moored in succession along our adjoining piers and (2) installed state-of-the-art windows at low cost, our grip on power started to wane.

As the backlash grew, the tactics used to attack our creditability were brilliant. It was also reminiscent of the right wing's propaganda machine in the 1960s and to this day.

Although we helped keep the development affordable, well-run, crime free and functioning with integrity and were rewarded with election victories year after year, we couldn't withstand the insidious tactics of some old-time residents to regain the reins of power. They turned some of our neighbors against us by distorting our record and spreading lies about our corruptibility. We were not prepared for such an effective onslaught on our individual and collective character.

Their campaign to undercut our popularity didn't at first deter our continuing accomplishments. For example, the jail barge protests in 1992 involved hundreds of residents of GG and the surrounding neighborhood. I was asked to do something about the barges. The motivation of some residents was that our property values would be affected. My motivation was based on the fact that the jail barges were placed opposite an elementary school, and the teachers were complaining that the children were running up to the classroom windows to watch the prisoners play basketball on the roof of the barge. What is more, we resented the fact that the Koch administration did not take the required step of trying to get the approval of the District 3 Community Board. Also, we learned that the barge was transferred from the Wall Street area to our pier, and that infuriated us.

We had meetings with turnouts in the hundreds. As I chaired the meetings, Sheldon Silver, our state assemblyman, who later became speaker, would sit on one side of me, and Miriam Friedlander would sit on the other. They would speak to me but not to each other. This was due to the fact that while their electoral districts overlapped they were intensely opposed to each other ideologically and during election campaigns. Miriam was much more to the left and because she was so outspoken in standing up for her beliefs she was not popular among several of her less militant peers including Shelly.

That way of communicating with each other through me continued until one day, away from a meeting, I questioned Shelly about it, and he did finally speak with Miriam and she told me how pleased she was.

We continued to try to educate the participants by holding rallies attended by candidates for mayor, invited experts on all sides of the issue to meetings, testified at community board meetings, appeared on free access television, and met with Koch administrators. We thought we had triumphed when the first barge was sent to moor off Rikers Island. To our surprise a second barge appeared, and we revived our campaign, which sent the second barge to Rikers. This was quite a political victory as Queens Borough President Claire Shulman and the powerful Speaker of the City Council Peter Vallone Sr. opposed having the barges moored off their Borough.

2 Jail Barges To Be Closed And Removed
By SELWYN RAAB, Published: February 15, 1992/NYTimes
One barge, the Bibby Resolution, is docked in the East River at Montgomery Street.(housing) 380 inmates.

The floating jails have been highly unpopular with their neighbors in Greenwich Village and the Lower East Side since plans for docking them there were first announced in the late 1980s.

During this time Charlotte needed full-time care, and after serving eleven years on the board, I decided not to run again. Sig decided to stay on the board but gave up the presidency. Although we still maintained a majority on the board, and I did remain chair of 6BHC, not one of our supporters on the board was at that time willing to assume the presidency.

These decisions gave opponents an opportunity to promote their candidates by attacking us. As a result 6BHC became a target as elections were taking place, and candidates started to use false but populist tactics. One candidate made a promise to keep the development spotless. She said she was ashamed to bring her relatives to visit. This assertion received loud applause at candidate's night, despite the fact that Bernard Gurrin had set up a vigorous cleaning regime. This candidate, having been forced to resign previously from the board for bad practices, won and became president.

Another candidate ran on the theme that he would address the crime problem at GG. As far we could tell, there was no crime problem, and the candidate completely ignored the fact that some of us had completely eliminated the drug and car theft rings. Yet the candidate's message was well received. Soon after he won, he convinced the board to change the security guard company.

During this period more of those opposed to us were elected until finally they took control of the board. It was also during this period that we experienced three negative or questionable events or trends.

A huge, illegal apartment selling operation occurred: A fire in the management's office damaged residents' files and signaled the fire department to assign an investigator. The GG secretary and two residents were convicted and sentenced to prison. We wondered whether non-6BHC Board members were also involved but who managed to avoid prosecution.

Rumors were spread that 6BHC members were involved, and nothing could have been further from the truth. I spoke up at an annual meeting defending the 6BHC members who were on the board. My statement was well received.

When we no longer were in control, the following vendors were replaced: management, security, laundry machines, and painters. We wondered why those moves were necessary and if the reasons given were as stated.

A contract with the state for GG to generate our own energy, initiated by 6BHC, was canceled.

Gary Huth, one of our strongest leaders, decided to seek the presidency, and he succeeded. During his tenure he oversaw the installation of state-of-the-art, easy-to-clean windows at a very low price. Gary, who worked far out on Long Island as a New York State economist and had a long commute, arriving home at seven or eight o'clock at night, put in inordinate amounts of time to make sure the window project went well. He met with the consultant engineer and the foreman for months every Thursday morning at 8:30 a.m., causing him to come home even later those nights to make up the time. The job he did was excellent. He kept the cost down from initial offerings of $17 to $3 million. Once installed, the satisfaction level among the residents was high. Despite the fact that people who know Gary well would testify to his having the highest order of integrity, the opposing side accused him of taking money under the table. Sig was accused of having something to do with the pay-for-apartment scandal, and I was vilified as chair of 6BHC.

The truth of the matter was that none of the board members we supported ever asked for or received special privileges. The best example was that Gary Huth remained on the parking lot waiting list for twelve of the 16 years he was on the Board without putting pressure on management to place him ahead of the queue.

We did make mistakes: (1) I allowed someone to join 6BHC whose previous behavior was despicable as a member of the board who was removed by the city. I reluctantly acquiesced when she said that I would be her "probation officer" and that she would not act on behalf of 6BHC or the co-op without my approval. Even though she kept to her bargain, one of our stalwart members was so furious with me that she quit 6BHC. Others questioned my judgment and lost interest in 6BHC; (2) We didn't pay enough attention to quality-of-life details. For example, we didn't strongly convey to management that our sidewalks, benches, and windows needed repair.

When Sig Israel was president, he maintained control of board meetings, but the presidents we supported who followed him, though also of impeccable integrity and administrative competence, were reluctant to keep discipline during meetings. They allowed non-board members to speak before board members. Meetings became more and more unruly, and the attacks made against me, 6BHC, and the board members we supported tended to overshadow the planned agenda.

Flyers were distributed falsely accusing us of wanting to raise maintenance fees unnecessarily and alarming residents of actions and positions taken by 6BHC. When we raised questions about their decisions, they often became volatile and sometimes threatened violence. At a community meeting one of them, a board member, jumped over a table to attack someone who asked him an embarrassing question. Later, his teenage sons threatened an older man for raising a controversial question at the meeting; paint was smeared on the doors of two of our board members; and I was openly threatened with violence when I raised a question about the ethical behavior of another board member.

As they established influence and power, they replaced most of our contractors, starting with the Gurrin management team. It was evident that they identified Gurrin with 6BHC. We wondered again why such drastic changes were necessary, especially at a time when the Manhattan District Attorney's office reported that private gifts of money were paid to managements across the city by contractors.

What occurred could be seen as a microcosm of the broader trends in society: progressive groups take on the herculean tasks of dislodging and replacing deeply entrenched forces, expend tremendous amounts of energy, sacrifice precious time, become exhausted, and are unable to withstand a backlash and a loss of political power.

In regard to lessons learned, as I have chaired other committees, I have been careful about whom to recruit. Before recruiting someone who might be controversial, I am now more sensitive to the wishes of group members. Also, I have become quite skilled at convincing people whom we thought ill-suited for our group to find other situations more appropriate to their needs. In regard to the tactics used that questioned our character and our intentions, we were completely unprepared. It shocked us to learn that the goodwill we generated over the years could be undermined so easily by a populist campaign based on lies and deception. We ended our control of the board, however, knowing that we had accomplished a great deal:

- We found ways to keep GG affordable for years to come,
- Forced the Koch administration to remove two jail barges,
- Led in the dismantling of two criminal gangs, and
- Installed excellent, easy-to-clean windows at a reasonable price.

Most of the 6BHC members who served on the board were, by 2005, too ill or exhausted to run again. In addition, it became too difficult to recruit new residents with our philosophy who were willing to serve with the newly elected board members and without the support of 6BHC, which had disbanded.

Witnessing our replacements on the board by those who, for the most part, campaigned with mischaracterization and intimidation and then governed with questionable practices, caused me initially to feel defeated. That soon faded when I reminded myself that we had a terrific run, and what we put into place has kept GG affordable and quite livable now in my fifty-second year at GG. Some members of our core group still keep in touch and have great warmth, care, and respect for each other. Important to me was that I did succeed in keeping Chandy's spirit alive within me. I reinforced my conviction that I could effect change without being as radical as she had been. I continued to use this method with other small groups organized to confront injustice.

At My Ninetieth Birthday Party
Former GG Board Presidents and Trustees
And Fellow 6BHC Activists
From the Left: Sig Israel*, Milagros Huth, Elsa Quinones, me, Gary
Huth*, Nancy Bartow, Elizabeth Archer* (*former presidents)

Three

PIC

The Public Issues Committee
of the
The New York Society for Ethical Culture
(NYSEC)

*S*UMMING UP: This was one of the most productive experiences I have ever had, but to describe it in detail would require a mini-book and a half. In providing only the highlights, however, I have found it difficult to write it in a reader-friendly story line manner throughout. I hope, however, that those who lived through the experience with me and members of the nationwide ethical movement and all readers might feel a bonding with our mission, what we tried to do, and what we managed to achieve.

It was great fun, but you may have to read between the lines to imagine what I and others may have felt and struggled to work through.

This chapter is in three parts.

1. PIC's mission
2. Our cast of characters
3. What we tried and what we accomplished
4. The process:

This I have saved for the end of the chapter to compare it with the process of the highly successful environmental ethical action committee of our society

The Public Issue Committee's Mission

I became chair of the Public Issues Committee in 2007. Our mission, believe it or not, was to try to influence the agenda of the 2008 presidential election. Filled with chutzpah, I proposed that:

> *We seek and advocate for progressive issues that are popular across ideological lines: opposition to the war in Iraq, paid family leave, and paid sick leave. Others on the committee suggested child health insurance, Iran, global warming, and stem cell research*

PIC's Cast of Characters

Among our members was a socialist, Alan Gardner, whom I called "PIC's Resident Scholar." Alan could give a rich history of unionism or socialism at a moment's notice and had a wonderful sense of humor. Although he often wanted us to take a more left/scholarly position, his constant support inspired us.

I called Eric Volpe "Ethical Culture's Conscience," because he took courageous positions that few of us were brave enough to follow, even though they were profoundly ethical and admirable. Eric sometimes worked with me on proposals such as the Iran policy but he not only expressed his disagreement on other issues verbally and forcefully, he was extremely disappointed when I wouldn't agree with him wholeheartedly.

One of the problems had to do with his conception that I personally supported Obama and that Obama sometimes took an immoral position. For example, Eric thought it was unjust for the United States to kill Iraqis and that US troops should immediately leave Iraq. When I pointed out that one of the main reasons the United States stayed was that Obama could not win reelection if he withdrew precipitously, Eric refused to consider that a valid reason. My reasoning was (and is) that sometimes in order to prevent a far more unethical group from gaining power, we may have to take account of the public's judgment even if it is faulty.

Nevertheless, I had great respect for Eric, as we all did.

Pat Berens usually volunteered to edit my writing, and I probably wouldn't have been published except for her probing questions and suggestions, which I almost always accepted. Pat was also comfortable enough to remind me to set limits on my sometimes frantic level of activity. It felt good that someone noticed and was concerned.

JoAnn Mason's persona was that of utmost self-confidence. She was a person of clear convictions, independence, and impressive capabilities. She refused to join NYSEC because we rented space to a group she believed was unethical — a group she believed was homophobic. With great effort, and over a period of years, I and others convinced her that by joining, she could better influence NYSEC's policy, and she definitely did.

NYSEC would not have had three excellent leaders if it wasn't for JoAnn's role on the search committee of 2009. Unfortunately, she died a few years later of cancer at a time when she was so very happy, having moved to be with her children and grandchildren.

By the way, months before she died, she posted this on Facebook: "Abe Markman is the sexiest man I ever met." As you would expect, I was quite pleased but completely confused. For the most part we had a very good relationship, but she never gave me any reason to think she was attracted to me sexually.

Phyllis Harrison Ross, MD, the only African American on PIC and among the very few people of color at NYSEC, was a highly successful psychiatrist. Because of her excellent career performance she was appointed Commissioner of the New York State Board of Corrections with oversight of the health services and medical conditions in all the state's prisons.

Phyllis was also on the editorial board of the *Amsterdam News* and had the opportunity to interview Hillary Clinton, Barack Obama, and David Patterson, and she had success promoting some of PIC's ideas with them, especially Child Health Insurance and paid sick leave.

Despite a powerful, self-confident persona, Phyllis tended to question the extent and degree of her acceptance at Ethical Culture. She would often say if it weren't for me and David and Valerie Leiman, an interracial couple, she probably would leave NYSEC. We shared our hidden prejudices with each other, which strengthened the bond between us. She would greet me with, "Hi, brother Abe."

She was both openly self-critical and a carefully thought out and successful activist, particularly for local, progressive change.

After annual and magnificent tributes to Phyllis, she became much more comfortable at NYSEC. What impressed me the most about Phyllis was that, despite her brilliance and formidable abilities and considerable influence in the Cuomo administration, she welcomed constructive advice.

Maria Fridman was a long-time member of NYSEC with deep feelings for people who were mistreated or forgotten. She died in 2015, leaving a lifetime of service to the homeless and others in dire straits. Although she was frustrated with me at times because she would propose pressing human rights positions that I thought were beyond the scope of PIC's mission, like the tragedy of Darfur, she remained a loyal and committed member. When I turned her down, she took the issue directly to the board and won approval.

Although Charles "Chuck" Debrovner, MD, director emeritus of the board, was not a member of PIC, he wrote our proposal on stem cell research. He has been of great help to me on a personal level, and there is no doubt that he will go down in the history of NYSEC as one of our most dedicated, influential, and respected members.

Lee Loshak held a left-wing worldview and constantly had ideas for exciting programs and would work hard to implement them. As we found speakers and writers, however, who were critical of the union movement, Lee suffered, as he believed—-as we all did—that the union movement had been essential in improving the lives of workers.

Barry Snyder was a dedicated worker and produced a well-documented work book of resources and information.

Ken Gans was very helpful regarding global warming. He would often question our arguments on other issues but would always come back for more give and take.

Virginia Arnold and Nancy Ambruster were hardworking PIC committee members. In addition, they came downtown to the annual LOISADA Festival, on Avenue C—four or five times on the Sundays of the Memorial

Day weekend. They would sit for hours at our Lower East Side Call for Justice table and help promote our policies, positions, and petitions.

The street fare attracted thousands of people of widely diverse backgrounds. With their help we collected about three hundred signatures year after year for reform of the draconian drug laws and for abolition of the death penalty. These were deeply held positions of both Ethical Culture and the Call for Justice, but they were outside of PIC's particular agenda.

Though not a member of PIC, Bonnie Bean, one of the most beloved, admired, and talented members of NYSEC, was always ready to help. Andra Miller, despite becoming a hardworking president of NYSEC, was a great supporter and was always willing to pitch in.

A few other members of our society wanted to join PIC, and I became the person to tell them they could not. They tended to use attention-getting devices that interrupted our free-flowing discussions. Although they thought I was acting alone, most often I was reflecting the opinions of PIC members.

Despite saying no to them in as tactful way as I could, I still was accused by a few Ethical Culture members of violating our principles of being accepting of all human beings. What I did point out is that successful musical bands, teams, and committees choose participants who can contribute the most and can best fit in. I would usually refer those turned away to other activities of the society, and sometimes that did work.

UPDATE: Phyllis Harrison-Ross died in early 2017. I miss her as a sister. The memorial tribute to her was worthy of the far-reaching contributions she made to humanity.

What We Tried and What We Accomplished
On Paid Sick Days

I was motivated to help relieve the pressure on young working couples sometimes caring for both their children and their elderly parents. Also essential in our present-day economy was paid family leave and universal day care, but sick leave was being considered in the New York City Council, so I thought we should start there.

PIC members became very active with the New York Paid Family Leave Coalition, and we established strong relationships with the union leaders, women activists, and public officials who participated. So when Dr. Phyllis Harrison-Ross, a member of PIC, suggested that we ought to consider a Breakfast Forum on Paid Sick Leave, I thought we could pull it off.

This was one of our issues that Phyllis, a member of the Amsterdam News Editorial Board, discussed with the candidates. Following her interview with Barack and Michelle Obama during and after the 2008 campaign, they both made strong statements in support of paid sick leave.

Possibly motivated by the pronouncements of the first family, San Francisco, Seattle, and Washington DC were the first cities to enact paid sick leave legislation. Studies showed that businesses in those cities were not adversely affected.

Here is an updated excerpt from my Ethical Action Report circulated to members of the American Ethical Union, May 2013.

NYSEC Helps Promote Paid Sick Leave: A Personal Reflection

In November, 2008, the Public Issues Committee initiated the planning for a Breakfast Forum on Paid Sick Leave in New York City. I was confident that members of the NY State Paid Family Leave Coalition would be willing to come uptown because of the very positive relationship we established with them and most important the high regard they had for Ethical Culture.

When we learned that the district's Councilmember, now Manhattan Borough President Gale Brewer was the main sponsor of the paid sick leave bill we asked for a meeting with her and her office was happy to arrange it.

Pat Berens, Maria Fridman, and Lee Loshak accompanied me to her uptown office. While she let us know that although there was a preponderance of support in the City Council, Mayor Michael Bloomberg was opposed to paid sick leave and Speaker Christine Quinn refused to bring it up for a vote. We invited Gale to be on the Breakfast Forum panel and she willingly accepted.

In Gail Brewer's presence we realized anew that both being ethical, dedicated to helping those in need and achieving excellence are possible in one elected official.

Phyllis and another prominent NYSEC member, Jerry Chamlin, recruited Chuck Hunt the Vice-President of the Restaurant Association for the panel. He reluctantly agreed to participate but he wanted assurance that in expressing his opposition to paid sick leave no one would throw "tomatoes at me." In addition, I was able to convince Nancy Ploeger, President of the Manhattan Chamber of Commerce to join the dialogue.

Days before the event some PIC members and I spoke to one of the panelists, a highly committed union advocate for paid sick leave, to avoid a down and out food fight with the business leaders on the panel.

In addition, every council member was contacted, by phone, snail or e-mail or by visits to their district offices. As a result, sixty people attended representing elected officials, women's groups, unions, and businesses.

New York Council Speaker Christine Quinn's office sent an e-mail message wanting to know if she was invited to be on the panel or in the audience. I conferred with the leaders of the NYS Paid Leave Coalition and Gale Brewer. The political advisor of the Coalition thought that if the Speaker announced at the forum that she was against passage it might dampen the dialogue.

I replied to the e-mail saying that we would love to have the Speaker attend but the panel has been set for quite a while. A few days later Gale wrote that it was okay to invite the speaker to be on the panel but by then the matter had been settled.

On the morning of the Breakfast, JoAnn Mason, Bonnie Bean, and Pat Berens came in at 6 AM to decorate and set out the food. We had enough for expenses as we had held a series of fund-raising summer movies.

Ethical Culture Society Leader Anne Klaeysen welcomed the guests with her special grace. I then urged proponents and opponents to try to walk in each other's shoes in seeking a way to provide relief for workers under stress.

We recruited as moderator, a PBS Nightly Business News anchor and a vigorous and sometimes angry give and take ensued. *But despite being the most ambitious project PIC undertook we left thinking it was an utter failure!*

During the forum, Chuck Hunt was thoroughly criticized by the advocates and he walked out of the room saying he would never come back to Ethical Culture!! I felt awful and for months afterward it was stated by a NYSEC staff member and repeated over and over again that our attempt at a dialogue was a total failure.

I tried to set up a meeting at a neighborhood café with Chuck Hunt, and an advocate, and myself. He seemed to appreciate my suggestion but the advocate didn't think he could help improve our chances for passage of the bill.

We learned a few months later, however, that the give and take at the forum did actually bring both parties a step closer to an agreement. Gale Brewer credited me several times for insisting at the Forum that the advocates on the panel consider an idea presented by Chuck Hunt. He said he could agree to include sick days in a package of days off that employees earn each year.

What happened was that when the moderator and the other panelists were silent to what I thought was a concession by a prominent business leader I asked the advocates if they could consider such an idea. Gale said it was worth further exploration. I then asked Donna Dolan, Chair of the NYS Paid Family Leave Coalition what were her thoughts on Chuck Hunt's proposal, and she also said it was worth considering.

I later learned at a City Hall hearing that the Hunt suggestion had been included in a revised bill. Members of the Chamber of Commerce still could not accept the bill, but other members of the business community said the new provision brought both parties closer.

Three staff members of the Public Advocate, Betsy Gotbaum, had attended the PIC breakfast and shortly afterwards she introduced a bill against discrimination toward workers who needed to take sick days.

Despite several City Hall rallies, which we attended, Speaker Quinn still refused to allow it to come to the floor for a vote. In February, 2013, Gloria Steinem told the New York Times that she would not vote for Christine Quinn for mayor unless the Speaker allowed a vote on paid sick leave. What is more, every Democratic candidate for mayor except Quinn promised to support Gale's bill. To our delight, in March, 2013, the New York City Council passed a Paid Sick Days Bill with a veto-proof majority.

A few weeks later, I was surprised to receive a round of applause from a large room full of NYSEC members and guests when Richard Van Deusen, our treasurer, while presiding at an April, 2013 Sunday Platform program, reported that Gail Brewer spoke of my contribution to this important law. I wanted to shout out that others did so much to make this happen.

What had happened was that Dick and several other Board members of NYSEC had met Gale at an event. Gale was asked whether she credited NYSEC with a role in passing the bill. She said yes but particularly she credited Abe Markman.

In sixty years of activism I have been one among many who fought, lost and won several battles for social justice. It has been rare, however, that I have been singled out as playing an important role in such a victory.

Update: The "U.S. will require its contractors to provide paid sick leave: echoing city and state laws, the (NYC) rule will affect an estimate of 1.1 million workers."—*New York Times*, September 30, 2016.

At one of several City Hall rallies, members of Ethical Culture and the Call for Justice, Ken Gans, Bill Antalics, me, Hugh McGuire, and Nancy Ambruster.

In the scanned copy on the next page of Borough President Gale Brewer's letter, she wrote that my role was crucial to passage of this important benefit.)

OFFICE OF THE PRESIDENT
BOROUGH OF MANHATTAN
THE CITY OF NEW YORK

1 Centre Street, 19th floor, New York, NY 10007
(212) 669-8300 p (212) 669-4306 f

163 West 125th Street, 5th floor, New York, NY 10027
(212) 531-1609 p (212) 531-4615 f

www.manhattanbp.nyc.gov

Gale A. Brewer, Borough President

December 30, 2014

Abe Markman
Former Chair of Public Issues Committee
New York Society for Ethical Culture
675 Water Street, Apt 5-C
New York, NY 10002

To Whom It May Concern:

As the former New York City Councilmember who sponsored the recently passed Paid Sick Leave Bill, I am happy to state that Abe Markman as Chair of the Public Issue Committee of the New York Society for Ethical Colure played a crucial role in bringing Paid Sick Leave to millions of workers in New York City

Mr. Markman acted early by organizing a breakfast dialogue of advocates and opponents from the business community. Every Councilmember was contacted and asked if they supported the bill and received visits from committee members. During the dialogue, at the well-attended event, Mr. Markman skillfully brought both sides to agree on a potential compromise that was key to the eventual passage of the bill.

Sincerely,

Gale A. Brewer

On Paid Family Leave

New York State passed a paid family leave bill providing twelve weeks of paid leave, April, 2016.

Our Other Positions:

- Iraq: NYSEC opposed the war with our near-frozen bodies on a February day in 2002 before entry.

Then in 2008, with the war in full bloom and several of Iraq's neighbors refusing to help, PIC advocated for:

- The United States to announce that it did not intend, when hostilities ceased, to establish a permanent military presence or to
- Claim primary rights to Iraq's oil.

We thought taking these positions would be a welcome sign to Iraq's neighbors and lead to a better climate for diplomacy and help in ending the war and contributing to the peace. Our proposal was added to the American Ethical Union's position at the United Nations, which advocated for a concentrated diplomatic effort to end the war and ample resources for reconstruction after hostilities ceased.

- Iran: We opposed an invasion of Iran that was being considered.
- Advocated for Stem Cell Research
- Global Warming: We called for resources to replace oil and coal with clean energy at a level equal to the "Manhattan Project" that created the atomic bomb.

Whether we had an impact on these issues is unlikely, but it raises an interesting question. Almost all of our ideas were implemented more or less by either the Obama administration, New York City, or New York State (among many other cities and states). So, was this just serendipity, good anticipation of what governments would do, or did all of our ideas pierce the political ether?

Before we were accepted as an ethical action committee some NYSEC Board members resisted PIC's acceptance as an official committee. It was mainly due to the fact that we chose positions unexamined by the Board instead of those determined priorities for ethical action: the death penalty and the draconian Rockefeller Drug Laws.

After PIC ended as a committee we were happy to learn that most of our issues were included in a DVD used to attract new NYSEC members.

In all humility, I believe that Ethical Culture Founder Felix Adler would have been proud of us.

PIC Closes Shop

In 2010, after three and a half years of intensive effort, I decided to retire from PIC. I was tired, and the pace was affecting my health. Also, the other members agreed to end as a committee. When I told Bob Liebeskind, NYSEC's executive director, he said he was sorry because "PIC was our most important committee." Carol Chamlin, long time former chair of the all-important Sunday Program Committee, used the same words when I told her.

At a final luncheon, the group gave me a generous gift certificate for books at a popular far-left literary hangout. Maybe the one who chose that spot thought I needed to become more leftist myself. We ended the luncheon with my sharing how I felt about each of them. My brief descriptions above of each member should shed light on what I said.

Post PIC Activities

headquarters and partners of a very effective, local Climate Change Alliance.

Global Warming
An outline

1. With considerable help from Leader Curt Collier and President Andra Miller my climate change proposal was adapted by the American Ethical Union at its 2010 General Assembly. I then was authorized by the Assembly to lead a letter-writing campaign in support of the EPA's desire to control carbon emissions. The campaign was joined by Ethical Culture Societies in eight cities.

2. In 2011, I decided to reengage by initiating and chairing an ad hoc committee in support of a program sponsored by Bill McKibben, the founder of 350.org. He announced with great enthusiasm "The Moving Planet," a day scheduled for September 24, 2011.

   Several other people volunteered and, despite short-term disappointments, most of us who participated became members of the highly successful Environmental Stewardship Committee.

   With the brilliant leadership of Paula Claycomb, Monica Weiss, Mary Houts, Phyllis Kreuttner, and Vince Brancato, and with Leader/ environmentalist Curt Collier's guidance, the ESC has become an important fixture in our ethical action firmament.

3. Monica Weiss teamed up with 350.org and its affiliates (based on our recommendation they meet at NYSEC rent free). She was the sole member of our committee to help in planning and executing the

largest march on climate change ever-held in New York City. Four hundred thousand people attended.

Monica's unmatched leadership skills became visible as she arranged the pre-march forum at NYSEC the night before and our eight-hundred-seat auditorium was nearly filled. As a result we have become the headquarters and partners of a very effective, local Climate Change Alliance. It is this Alliance spear-headed by Lyna Hinkel of the local branch of 350.org that should be given major credit for New York City deciding to divest $5 billion from fossil fuels.

4. Vincent Brancato led NYSEC's contribution to the statewide campaign against fracking. Working in alliance with United against Fracking and other very effective organizations, the result was that Governor Anthony Cuomo banned fracking in New York State.

How Important Is the Process:PIC's:

- Found members willing through their expertise or interest to write one-page proposals.
- Scheduled a series of discussions of the proposals open to the entire NYSEC membership,
- Sought board approval. Once a position was endorsed by the board, it became the position of the society. Nevertheless, in order to involve our membership as fully as possible, we sought and
- Obtained ratification at an annual membership meeting
- Became well-informed advocates for these positions

Some members and I vowed to promote the PIC process.

The committee's recommendation was that the "PIC Process" should be used when confronting ethical action issues. NYSEC has members who have the people skills for an action-oriented fellowship, the expertise for research, the contacts to attract speakers or choose relevant documentaries, and a wide array of advocacy skills. In addition, issues became so well-crafted that members became knowledgeable and willing participants in our campaigns.

Environmental Stewardship Committee

I must agree, with Vince that his and Monica's methods of concentrating more heavily on alliances with well-defined action agendas not only paid huge dividends, it required less energy.

Although they did and are still doing a fantastic job they educated our membership more so through films, large forums, and a few humongous rallies. Though we used those methods on a smaller scale we were more intimately involved with more of our members in decision-making and in taking a variety of actions on the ground.

My conclusion is that both methods are valid in different circumstance and with different players.

Or, if you want to avoid the kind of exhaustion I achieved after chairing PIC for three and a half wonderful years, choose the Vince and Monica way to go. I applaud them and appreciate the fact that I can participate with them and not work so hard.

Four

Accepting the Community Service Award

Sunday, January 31, 2010

Gale Brewer, the borough president of Manhattan, and Reverend Afiya Dawson, who was my partner during many of our workshops with black teenagers and young adults on what to do when stopped by the police, spoke first. Both were effusive in their praise. So too was Phyllis Harrison Ross, M.D. but she intermixed the praise by saying that "Abe is brilliant despite the fact that he is so old and s-o s-l-o-w in his responses."*

A Few Excerpts
From My Remarks

I want to thank Alex Mogieleff for suggesting this, the board of trustees for deciding to do it, the awards committee for having to deal with this cantankerous old man, Sheila Kleinwald for going well beyond anyone's expectations in making the luncheon arrangements, members of my family, and members of the LES Call or Justice and fellow warriors of Gouverneur Gardens where we live.

Besides my family there are three groups that should be standing up with me. Would all of my neighbors from Gouverneur Gardens, the Lower East Side Call for Justice, and members of Public Issues Committee please stand.

And now I want to ask my family to stand. I want them to know how proud I am of every one of them. As the last living member of my generation, I constantly tease them by saying there is no one left who can dispute any of my bubba maysas. A bubba maysa is Yiddish for tales that are hardly true in fact but mostly true in spirit. And now I'll keep quiet until I see you at lunch.

*Note: I insisted that the planned toast for me at lunch be a roast as well. Phyllis Harrison-Ross couldn't attend the luncheon and so she told me that she would roast me during her morning remarks. Although what she said about me being slow was in good humor it was an example of how much we knew about and trusted each other. At the luncheon, family and friends told of my being a pain and a nudge but that I meant well and sometimes was on target.

PART IV
The Color of Reaction

East Harlem in the 1960s: A Personal Odyssey

Originally delivered in September, 2009 as a platform address at the New York Society for Ethical Culture.

In November 2008, I was interviewed on radio station WBAI. The program was sponsored by our Ethical Culture Society and was called Ethics-on-the-Air. A caller asked me a difficult question, and I didn't have enough time to answer it.

The question was, "How can you have empathy for the man you described who was so wrong?" The caller was referring to the prototypical angry white man of the 1960s who I described. One of the reasons this man was angry was that a family of color moved into his all-white neighborhood. But he was upset about many other things happening during that turbulent era. In the 2008 election cycle, he is the white working-class man without a college education that all the presidential candidates are trying to reach. The way he and women with similar attitudes vote in November might determine who wins the White House and the Congress. (Now we know.)

This talk is dedicated to answering the caller's question more fully.

The angry man I referred to is a composite of a working-class and middle-class man, who in the 1960s and 1970s led a relatively insulated, traditional life. He had a wife and a teenage daughter and a young adult son. During a short ten-year period, a black family moved next door, his teenage daughter became sexually active, his wife spoke of her need for fulfillment beyond the home, his son refused to fight for his country, a nephew came out of the closet, a close relative went through a divorce, a friend of his daughter died of a drug overdose, riots occurred in major cities, and leaders in society were assassinated. On top of that, his income declined to the point that his wife had to find employment outside the home. This led to his children getting less care and protection in the home.

Even if we cannot find one man who went through all of this, just living through an era when such things could happen to him and his friends would be enough to cause him deep distress and intense, sustained anger. He blamed liberals because he felt that while they were marching and protesting for their rights and the rights of others, they were trampling on his rights and ignoring his needs and the needs of his family.

Finding the empathy within oneself for someone whose attitudes are so foreign from your own is very difficult. An essential tool is the imagination to live in their skin with their strongly ingrained attitudes. It also might require experiencing an era of intensive change that we are not fully equipped to handle ourselves.

Here is the story of how I developed understanding for the man I described above. Working in East Harlem from 1962 to 1976 as Program Director of the Washington Houses Community Center of Union Settlement, I was in some ways treated as if I was that kind of man. Here are just a few of the challenges I either was forced to face or chose to face:

- Militant activists campaigned to take over the youth program that I ran.
- Staff and parents were in denial of my assertion that drug abuse was spreading among the young people.
- Staff, parents, neighborhood leaders, and the youth themselves fervently lobbied me to allot federally funded summer youth jobs as a welfare benefit. They wanted me to ask for as many slots as possible and fill them whether there was a real task for the young people to perform or not.

I refused and limited the number of slots that we took. I insisted on assigning the teens to real jobs, for example, as a counselor-in-training or a teacher's aide in one of the settlement's three large day-care centers. In addition, there had to be a supervisor available, and the young people had to have the capacity to learn how to do that job.

I was vindicated when the Union Settlement staff assigned to supervise the youth spoke well of them and complimented me for placing them in their programs. In contrast they stressed that they were assigned other teens from surrounding neighborhood community centers that were not nearly as motivated or effective as those teens I sent them. The other neighboring community centers took on many more teens in addition to those they referred to our several programs but did not assign them to real jobs, and so the young people often whiled away their time with little or nothing to do.

- Gang members I knew joined the riot following the assassination of Dr. Martin Luther King Jr. When I heard that they were involved, I wondered what they were up to and so I looked for them. I found them on Third Avenue and 104th Street. It was a wild scene, but when they saw me they gathered around and let me know what they were planning to do. They told me they were going to turn over a police car. I succeeded in talking them out of it but I wondered what they would do when I left. (No police car was reported to have been up-ended.)

These experiences tested my and my staff's attitudes and abilities to grow. As Black Americans and Latinos they sometimes over-identified with the members and sometimes I had to act without their support or even in the face of their resistance. However, Center Director Alice Suzuki was a tower of strength and shared her great wisdom, experience, and resolve when I needed it the most.

While facing these enormous social problems in my professional life, my neighbors on the Lower East Side were calling my wife, daughter, and me "The Revolutionaries." It was because of our activism in the community. This was not known to the teenage and young adult members of the Union Settlement community center I served.

So, here is the story of how I could have been considered a revolutionary in my personal life and a reactionary at work. Here is how my two parallel universes came together and how I developed the empathy for working-class white people with mind-sets utterly opposed to my own.

On the day that Martin Luther King Jr. was killed, I called a meeting of the young members of the center. They filled our lounge and sat in a large circle. I told them how upset I was and wondered how they were feeling. Before they could answer an African American staff member spoke up in a militant way. He blurted out that "Passive nonviolence died with Martin Luther King." I strongly disagreed and said, "You left out an important word. That word is resistance." I pointed out that the passive resistance of nonviolent, civil disobedience was particularly suited to the Deep South. I said it would have been suicidal to use violence there and even in the North and nonviolence did succeed in changing the entrenched attitudes of many people.

After that session several of the black high-school age members came to me, the only white person on staff, and asked if I would set aside time on a regular basis to rap with them. I was happy to do that and in these sessions, I spoke to them about issues like the Vietnam War and showed them a film about the lies that were being told about it. I said they had a choice. It was the choice not to serve. They could try to get a college deferment and I told them how they could register as conscientious objectors and took them in busloads to participate in youth conferences. I thought the conferences would help them better understand the tremendous peer and societal pressures they were living with. They were being pressured to take drugs, become sexually active, join a gang or the Black Panthers or Young Lords, sign up early for the war, or cover up their homosexuality. Adults caved in under such pressures and some of the youth were caving in as well.

At one of these conferences, the speaker, a black social worker who I deeply respected, made an outrageous statement. He wanted the young people to know that there was black knowledge and white knowledge and that the young people should only listen to or read books by black authorities. I spoke up and said that there is no such thing as black or white knowledge. What is true — is true — no matter the source.

A white staff member from Hudson Guild, who I once worked with, came up to me after the conference and said I should not have contradicted the speaker. Her reaction was typical of the intimidation many whites were experiencing.

Back at the center, a college student and an older brother of one of the young people in the group invited a few of his classmates to the center. One told me that he was a member of the Black Panthers and wanted to join the rap sessions. He named himself after a French revolutionary. Let's call him Pierre. He was a brilliant and charismatic young adult but whose tactics were so extreme that I came to doubt that he was really a Panther. Another classmate, let's call him Carlos, said that he was a member of the Young Lords.

At the rap sessions, Pierre brought literature about Leninism and asked the members and me if we could read passages for discussion. I made it clear to Pierre that I had no objection so long as there was an opportunity to express other opinions.

Pierre told me that the way to bring about revolutionary change was to duplicate what the Algerians did in their successful revolution against France. The Algerian militants believed that it was the drug kingpins and dealers that were working hand-in-hand with and protecting the colonial government. Before the native Algerian revolutionaries could secure a political opening to take over that government their strategy was to get rid of the purveyors of illegal drugs. And they did just that by going into the streets. First, they beat up the dealers, and then they got rid of the drug power brokers. The path was cleared to remove the French-controlled government and take over the reins of power.

With that strategy in mind, at one of our rap sessions, Pierre told our members that they needed to do the same. I said that was outrageous and highly dangerous. I could see the shock on faces of the teens he was to trying to convince but they did not say anything at the time.

A day or two later, a few of the older teens came to see me and said they wanted to tell me something but that I had to promise not to share it with Pierre. The night before, Pierre wanted them to join him in beating up a white man sitting on a bench outside the center. The man looked like he was high on heroin. They refused and the man was left alone. I was amazed and I praised them for standing up to Pierre.

One afternoon Pierre showed up and wanted to use the duplicating machine. He wanted to copy a flyer announcing a meeting at this community center exclusively for people of color. I told him that everyone in the community has to be invited to public meetings and that he could not use the machine. He said I was causing him a lot of trouble.

I told him that he was the one causing trouble as he was intimidating the young people. I told him that a few of the younger members came to me and said they were signing up for the military even if they had to go to Vietnam. They said it was too difficult for them on the streets. They said it as if they were apologizing to me.

I tried to figure out a way to reach Pierre and his clique of college students. They told me that if I wanted acceptance from them I would have to act like John Brown and put my life on the line just as he did to end slavery in America. I was frustrated but it finally dawned on me to deal with them just as I did with street gangs. I remembered that gang members were much more likely to open up away from their peers.

An opportunity came when Pierre told me in detail about an incident he had with the police. It was obvious that he provoked the police unnecessarily. I tried to help him see that. Although he didn't respond, he did listen carefully to me. I told him I would be willing to go to the hearing with him. He turned me down but I felt I had touched a sensitive chord.

In the meantime, without telling me in advance, a group of mostly white staff members in Union Settlement's main building, which is six blocks from the Community Center, and who only had a glimmering of what was happening, organized an informal discussion. They called it "The New Breed." Pierre was the guest speaker and proved quite a hit. When he said that his goal was to take over the running of the program at the center I lost my temper. I yelled out, "That will never happen."

Back at the Center, I learned that Pierre without permission was going to call for a large meeting just for people of color. The Center director and I agreed to close the Center the night of the meeting and we alerted some of the parents. That night Pierre stood before the door and said, "Let's break the glass panel and get in." The parents who showed up told him, in no uncertain terms, that he could not do that. They said, "This is our Center and we will not allow you to damage it."

Pierre came to see me the next day in a furious state and asked me why I closed the center. I reminded him that he could not arrange meetings without our permission and especially if whites were not allowed to attend.

I asked him why he was turning his revolution against me as I was the one who allowed him to have a forum at the center. He revealed to me that he was just following orders and he didn't expect to live much beyond the age of twenty-one. Interestingly, I used to get the same response from gang members on the Lower East Side. He asked if we could work together to have a meeting open to all about the use of drugs in the neighborhood. I agreed.

In the meantime, the Young Lord, Carlos, came to me and said that if I wanted to gain their respect I should involve people who supported me in the community to come and speak up for what I have meant to them. I wondered why I hadn't thought of that myself. I thanked him, and went out and did just that. As a result, during our large meeting on drug addiction, African American and Latino young adults who I had helped through several difficulties in the past came in large numbers and spoke up. They made strong statements refuting Pierre when he accused whites of being the sole movers and shakers of the drug trade. They said that both whites and people of color were behind it and that both whites and people of color were leaders of the new drug treatment programs, namely, Phoenix, Odyssey, and Exodus House–type programs.

A day or two later, a remarkable thing happened. Carlos came to me with a *Daily News* photo of me on the front page opening up a school on the Lower East Side. It was during the teacher's strike of 1968. He congratulated me and said, "See Abe, you needed to be revolutionized and we succeeded. We revolutionized you! And so we are not needed here anymore."

Pierre and Carlos left the center and there was no more talk of taking over the program. A few months later, I met Pierre on East Broadway not far from where I lived. He looked frantic and under stress. He said his group was thinking of taking over a partially abandoned tenement across the street. That was the last time I ever saw him and wondered if indeed he would live past twenty-one.

Thirty-two years later, in the year 2000, I did run into several of the African American young men who in 1968 asked me to rap with them and their Latino friends. It was in East Harlem at a Union Settlement affair. I was about to leave when they surrounded me for about forty-five minutes and they wouldn't let me go. They were then in their late forties and early fifties. They said they couldn't tell me as teens how much I meant to them but they could tell me now. They told me I was more important in their lives then their own parents and that I had helped them more than I could ever know. It was an experience I will never forget.

Nevertheless, thinking of that earlier time and being a white person whose attitudes were tested over and over again during that fourteen-year period was a profound learning experience. I understood how it felt when your core values were constantly challenged. My social work training and life experiences helped tremendously but I became aware of the emotional upheaval that the white working-class man must have gone through, a man who had much less education and training than I had. I had empathy for him because I understood how difficult it would have been for that man to accept the social revolutionary changes of that era. He felt that he and his family were forced to live in a new world. It was a world he didn't like at all. And it was a world he was determined to change back to what it was before the 60s.

So, you might ask the question in what way have I used that empathy. For years following my work in East Harlem, I did research to find progressive programs that would be acceptable and beneficial to most working men and woman. These would be programs supported by both the stay-at-home-oriented families who no longer could afford to stay at home with their kids and career-oriented families.

I believe that working men and women today of all political persuasions see the necessity of joining together on the issues that affect all of us.

UPDATE (1), Including Notes on Trumpism:

Isn't the angry white man of the TRUMP era experiencing inner turmoil similar to the Reagan Democrat whom I described above, except that now men and many women are experiencing cultural and economic change at an even more overwhelming intensity and pace?

PART V
The Color of Service

One

THE WILTWYCK SCHOOL FOR BOYS

As indicated, my first full-time job after finishing college in 1951 was at the Wiltwyck School for Boys in upstate New York. I was counselor to eleven, ten-year-old boys remanded to this camplike setting by the courts. After struggling unsuccessfully for one full year to gain control of my group, I decided to leave. While waiting for the train to take me home from Wiltwyck, an older black fellow counselor joined me. He then admitted to being a player in one of the most astonishing stories in race relations I ever experienced. As indicated he told me that he, with the other black counselors, were quite impressed that I stayed for a full year. He said most white counselors stayed for two weeks, and he admitted that their early departure was most often caused by the carefully worked-out plan of his fellow black male counselors.

They had a secret pact. They formed it when the African American executive director, Robert L. Cooper, for whom they had great respect, was fired and replaced by a white man from Austria, trained in Freudian psychoanalysis. They were outraged that a highly effective black administrator was supplanted by a foreigner whose method of disciplining the young boys was as alien to them as the new executive himself. He constantly talked of discipline based on the boy's particular form of misconduct. He called it "consequences." So, if a boy stole something, it was appropriate to take something from him and then ask him how he felt about being deprived of a valued possession. What he valued was kept from him until he showed authentic contrition. When the new executive director left us for his New York City office, the staff would have a session of ridicule and laughter about "consequences."

Twelve of the senior black counselors in league with one white older European-born woman plotted to undermine the ability of newly appointed counselors to function. As all the new hires were white, it could have been seen as the racism of blacks against whites, but you can decide that when you read the story in full. I mention it here for two reasons:

1) It was an example of the considerable staying power I had. Almost all of the other new counselors left after days of the insidious undermining of their service to their group. Only one other white counselor hired during my stay remained for more than a full year. He was accepted as he was able to control his group. He was as cold and indifferent to me as were the others.

   They decided that they would do everything they could to undermine the new administrator's performance. Their major technique was to incite the boys in each group to explode in misbehavior as soon as their new counselor was left to manage them without a mentor.

I had been attracted to apply for a job at Wiltwyck when I visited with my undergraduate sociology class. Here were preteens, remanded to Wiltwyck for being unmanageable and were leisurely fly-fishing peacefully in the river with their counselor, Clarence Cooper. Clarence was featured in the award-winning film *The Quiet One*. The day of our visit, he was living up to the role he played in the film as a counselor of boys who related to him with warmth and respect.

Clarence was also, the younger brother of Robert L. Cooper, the former director, and also the counselor assigned to introduce me to my group.

When I joined him, he and the boys were lounging on their cots, playing games with each other quietly. After a few minutes an older female counselor appeared. Clarence introduced me to her and said that she was quite experienced and would continue my orientation for two weeks. Within minutes after Clarence left, she gasped for air and pointed to her heart. It was notice-ably pulsating. She said she had to leave for the clinic and that I was in charge.

Within a half hour after she left, and without my saying or doing anything that could possibly have provoked them, the boys broke forty-five windows and started a fire. In addition, I found one boy in the snow up to his knees, yelling about something I could not understand.

As Wiltwyck was organized with buildings either attached or close to one another, I am sure other counselors could hear the clamor, but no one came to help me. When the boys gathered for bed, I asked them what their rampage was all about, and they did not respond.

I later learned that the woman, who was supposed to show me the ropes, had been on the Austrian stage and that she had convinced the boys that she had magic powers, and that is how she controlled them.

Being naïve and inexperienced, I thought their behavior was due to their loss of Clarence until I met the counselor on the train going back to New York.

2) Another reason I tell this story is that by the time I met Charlotte, I had an intense experience living and working with African Americans. Although it was a negative one in a major way, I did establish some positive lasting relationships and gained some valuable insight.

It was a most difficult year for me as I tried to gain control of the group. In one incident the boys were found on the other side of the Hudson River by the police. When our director was called to get them, he asked them how in the world they crossed the river. They said they followed the deer tracks left in the snow and ice across the Hudson, which was quite wide at that location.

The second white female on staff was the art therapist. When she left Wiltwyck and returned to her own distinctive artwork full time, she was still so devoted to the school that she organized what she called the "Wiltwacks." Former staff and boys formerly in residence were invited to alumni-type gath-erings at several annual meetings.

At one of those upbeat affairs, I met a young adult who had been in my group. He told me that he had become a winning professional boxer. This was the same young man whom I once had disciplined by taking him from his bed and insisted that he stay outside the building until he calmed down. What he did was go to the program director's cabin and complain, at which point the director spoke quite tactfully to both of us to work things out in other ways.

Though I was vehemently against boxing, I was glad that he was doing well in a career that he loved. I also wondered whether he took to boxing because he wasn't able to challenge me physically when I carried him out of the cabin when he was ten years old. By the way, he was following Floyd Patterson, the world boxing champion and later head of the New York State Athletic Commission, who was at Wiltwyck long before my time.

Despite my difficulties, I met some counselors who were friendly. It took several more jobs with acting-out youth, however, for me to realize that my inability to set limits was not a winning trait with troubled youngsters.

On reflection I realized these African American men who rebelled against the new administration at Wiltwyck walked with military posture, dressed well and appropriately, and were self-respecting and very competent. There was some corporal punishment but it was carried out as if it were an accepted tradition. The boys in their care behaved well, and some graduated and had successful careers. Besides Floyd Patterson, Claude Brown, author of *Manchild in the Promised Land*, was a Wiltwack as well. According to Wikipedia, "… (the book) sold more than 4 million copies and has been translated into 14 languages."

The men were impressive father figures to all the boys in their care but they reminded me of the people described by E. Franklin Frazier in his book *The Black Bourgeoisie*. These men were so much like those I learned so much about in later years from Charlotte. They lived up to the image she wove by projecting a self-confident but superior attitude.

For example, during the first few nights after starting, they set me up playing the card game 21 for money. I can't recall exactly how it worked, but it was five of them against me, and when I ran out of money they ended the game without showing any emotion. And for the rest of the year, they hardly ever spoke to me.

This experience was a blow to my self-image. On hearing the whole story, however, I was at first astonished and then felt better about myself.

Unfortunately, the youngsters entrusted in our care were exploited by the "games" that the staff played. Nevertheless, I had no awareness of my true role with them until I was on my way home.

Two

The Neighborhood Self-Help Older Persons Project

(N-SHOPP)
Some Highlights

I co-founded the Neighborhood SHOPP in 1980 with Magdalen "Maggie" Garvin in 1980. Maggie was a wonderful partner. She would tell people, "Abe is the philosopher and I am the organizer," and was she ever! Maggie died several years ago, and I dedicate this chapter to her.

When I retired in 1995, the budget in this Bronx-based social service agency was $250,000. It has grown tenfold and is now $2,500,000. N-SHOPP serves predominantly African American and Latina older adults in groups and individually in several parts of the borough, often quite a distance from our office on Southern Boulevard in the South Bronx.

N-SHOPP's Prehistory
In 1976 I was hired by the Tremont Improvement Program Neighborhood House (TIP), a settlement house in the South Bronx, to administer a three-year grant from the Edna McConnell Clark Foundation. The aim was to involve older people in traditional volunteer services, for example, as aides in public schools and day-care centers.

As program director, however, I was given the option to rewrite the grant without changing its aim. Instead of traditional volunteering, I proposed that the older people in this South Bronx community would be more at home in self-help, mutual-aid, educational, and service projects.

When the E. M. Clark Foundation grant supervisor, also named Clark but who was not related to the sponsors, read my proposal, he said it was very interesting but it sounded more like a senior center program rather than a volunteer initiative. Nevertheless, he allowed me to go ahead with my concept. One of our first projects was what I call: "A Civil War Secret."

In the West Farms Section of the Bronx there is a soldiers' cemetery. It was surrounded by the Phipps Houses, a nonprofit, low-rent housing development that won an architectural award. Phipps officials sponsored and heavily funded TIP and sat on its board.

In 1976 when I came to work at TIP as a community social worker, the residents living around the cemetery were almost all African American. The war of 1812 graveyard was cared for by two elderly white history buffs. They came to me, frustrated that no one was willing to help them care for what they considered hallowed ground. They wondered what would happen to the cemetery when they could no longer keep it in good condition.

I suggested that they might consider transferring the body of a black soldier interred in Arlington National Cemetery. In that way members of the black community might identify with what would no longer be considered only gravestones of white soldiers who fought in a little-known war.

One of the men, Mr. S., was enraged at my suggestion. As a grandnephew of a Civil War soldier, he knew that was impossible and acted like I should have known better. His friend Mr. M., however, came to me a few weeks later and said he knew of a black woman who spied for the North in the Richmond, Virginia, home of Jefferson Davis, the president of the Confederacy. Her name was Mary Elizabeth Bowser. She was a freed slave placed in the Davis home by the daughter of her former owner. The daughter was a tried-and-true abolitionist.

Mr. M. said his own daughter had planted a tree in his backyard to be dedicated to him upon his death. He wanted to plant the tree in the soldier's cemetery and dedicate it to Mary Elizabeth Bowser.

The community was thrilled with the idea. Money was raised for a plaque. Well-attended annual ceremonies were held for this little-known Civil War hero. A highlight of the ceremonies was Mr. S. strutting about in his grand-uncle's Civil War uniform and then coming to attention and standing erect. The 150-year-old sword he proudly leaned on was almost as tall as he was. As a result of these joyous occasions, several children and parents volunteered to help Mr. S and Mr. M. with the cemetery.

One of the reasons Mary Elizabeth Bowser was hardly recognized in history was that her family, continuing to reside in Richmond, Virginia, the former capital of the Confederacy, kept her story secret for several generations in order to protect them. We were surprised and excited when on October 16, 1977, the Richmond News Leader noted: "A tree was dedicated yesterday at the West Farms Soldiers Cemetery in the Bronx, in honor of Mary Elizabeth Bowser. Organizers of the tribute hope to trigger national recognition for Miss Bowser, who they say played a vital role in the Union's victory at Richmond, VA in 1864."

We tried in other ways to "trigger national recognition" of this utterly courageous and heroic woman by contacting her descendants. I reached an articulate, elderly relative of Ms. Bowser by phone, living in Richmond. She refused to have a conversation with me about her long-deceased forebear. Her response seemed to confirm that the family from the Civil War to the day of my call in 1977 continued to believe that it was dangerous to speak about their relative, someone who may have affected the trajectory of the bloodiest war in our history.

Shortly after our ceremonies, Maggie did extensive research and wrote a script about Ms. Bowser, which I think was sent to and rejected by PBS. We then learned that a US general was conducting research about Bowser, and within a year, PBS did mention this remarkable woman in a documentary. I asked Maggie if it sounded like her script. She was not sure, but she looked disappointed that didn't receive credit for her research.

Since then Bowser has received some recognition in the literature: "In 1995 the U.S. government honored Mary Elizabeth Bowser for her work in the Civil War with an induction into the Military Intelligence Corps Hall of

Fame in Fort Huachuca, Arizona" (Hutchens Center for African-American Research).

In an age of tearing down statues in homage to the Confederacy, when will it become possible to fully acknowledge and celebrate nationally the unparalleled courage of a freed black female spy who voluntarily returned to slavery in order to help bury it?

Less than a year after the visit from Mr. Clark, we invited him to hear the story of the cemetery but principally for a tour of the ten gardens that were started and run by the seniors in various locations within a mile or two of the Tremont/West Farms section.

With the help of government-sponsored truckloads of topsoil, women who grew up on farms in the South and in Puerto Rico grew vegetables that most people thought could not be grown in the abandoned, debris-filled lots near their buildings.

In one garden they grew collard greens, corn, and tomatoes. A few men watching the gardeners spent their days drinking wine and looking like they might break into the garden. So the group's older adult female leader invited them to take some of the vegetables in return for watching the garden when it was closed, and that worked out well for all.

We told Mr. Clark that we had recently organized a caravan of private cars and the project's own van, visiting all the gardens and ending with a festival in the largest one. He was quite impressed.

A few months later, after he learned of our pioneering wellness program in affiliation with a nursing school, the pioneering gardening, and the Mary Elizabeth Bowser ceremonies, he returned for a meeting with our board president and told him that our program was the most creative of the many older adult volunteer programs funded nationwide by his foundation.

We discovered and helped form the N-SHOPP groups, mostly of black and Latina women, aged sixty and older, residing in housing for the elderly, low-rent housing, a walk-up tenement, and a church. Housing managers and ministers gave us free space in return for our provision of programs for their residents and congregations. We continued to recruit groups, and by the third year, we had enlisted twelve self-help groups.

Our process was to start with programs familiar to the older adults, choose leaders from each group to form a leadership council, move to more interpersonal levels of self, community and intergenerational services requiring more training and adventures in learning and teaching in more difficult service projects. Groups often decided to start with teaching each other sewing, crocheting, and macramé.

They became quite good and especially after we enrolled the teachers in the excellent Elder Craftsmen Program. Groups then moved to the gardening and the highly successful wellness program.

By the end of the third and final year of funding from the Clark Foundation and despite raising small grants from the Public Welfare Foundation and corporations, we had no prospects to continue. The Phipps Houses, Inc., the sponsor of TIP, was only willing to carry us for a while.

We invited all of our groups to the TIP Community Center to report on the wonderful work we did together and to tell them the program would probably end soon if we could not find more funds. It was ninety degrees Fahrenheit outside, and it felt hotter inside because of a huge turnout. I put my heart and soul into that speech.

Unbeknownst to me one of the seniors brought Assemblyman Louis Nine to the meeting. After I spoke he came to me and said, "Call me, and I will help you." I had always shied away from seeking funds from politicians, so I didn't call him for a month or two. The Phipps executives who were on TIP's Board, despite loving our program, told us that they couldn't continue to fund N-SHOPP. So I called Louis Nine, and he said, "How much do you want, and when do you want it."

Although he thought my request of $150,000 was reasonable, he wanted to meet someone who could assure him that we were a well-considered and trustworthy program. Mr. Clark was happy to meet with him. He came to Louis's office in the heart of the South Bronx, groomed like a high financier, and spoke highly of us and what we had achieved.

Once we received the authorization for the grant, the assemblyman, after reviewing our budget, came to see me at TIP with his top staff person. He pointed to the line item for a social group worker salary at $15,000. He said,

"I want you to break that up into two jobs with a salary of $7,500 each. They would be assigned to knock on doors and find out what services people need and want." I knew immediately that he wanted them to be foot soldiers in his reelection campaign.

I reminded him that I brought Mr. Clark to see him with the conviction that I would be allowed to continue a program that he had thought well enough to fund. I said, "Let me run the program, and I will do everything to help the seniors and make us all feel proud."

He said, "That is very interesting," and he left.

I told this to a Latino board member of TIP, and he said, "Abe, I admire you for your stand, but you will probably never get another grant from Louis Nine."

Nevertheless, Louis became a booster of our program and a supporter for three more years until he died. As an example of the trust he had in me, he convinced a group of highly educated older adult Puerto Ricans, who wanted to prove they could set up an ethnic library without help from non-Puerto Ricans, to invite me to help them get state funds through the pipeline so they could start their library. With a bit of advice from me and their own brilliance, they did get their funds.

Here is what led to Maggie and me to cofound N-SHOPP as a nonprofit independent of TIP: A black militant construction crew took over TIP's premises. They wanted the white executive director, who was a staunch supporter of Maggie and me, to restore the job of a popular black children's program worker she had fired. (I can't remember the reason for his dismissal but it seemed reasonable when it was explained to me.)

The construction crew had a reputation for violence, and when they ordered us to leave the building, the TIP staff, most of whom were black, did not resist. I picked up the phone to call 911, and a woman who was in the crew disconnected it and pushed me hard toward the door. The police, however, figured out the essence of my message because they showed up.

When they came, we were standing in front of the building, and the black staff advised me not to say anything out of fear that someone might get hurt. When the police asked who called, I told them it was me. They asked if I wanted the building opened, and I said yes. As I walked toward the padlocked door with the police, the leader of the construction crew came to me and said in a somewhat threatening voice, "I do not recommend that you open the building."

I said, "I will not if you allow us to get the milk out for the kids before it spoils." He let us do that if I promised not to try to enter again. He accepted my word and the incident was over for the moment. This was the first of several events that led to our leaving TIP:

The executive's curt firing of the black worker was an important factor that led to her own dismissal.

1. She was replaced on a temporary basis by someone I had supervised when he was a social work student intern at Union Settlement in East Harlem.

2. I was then asked to be on the search committee for the ongoing executive director position, and I should have known better. My former student was competing with someone I couldn't support. Both were black, but I sensed that the new candidate might be intolerant of me as a white person under his supervision. It seems so obvious now that I should not have trusted all the others on the committee when I spoke out against hiring him. As soon as he started, he made it clear that the previous independence Maggie and I had to run N-SHOPP according to our best professional judgment was over. For example, without consulting with me, he wanted Maggie to split her job with a young black female social worker.

Though she was a capable worker whom I had hired, she was not nearly as experienced as Maggie. He also made it clear that he didn't like the self-help emphasis of our program. He favored casework or a one-on-one service model. When at his first staff meeting he dismissed, in a blunt manner, a manual of personnel practices the board asked me to write, thus undermining my role at TIP, it became crystal clear that we were no longer welcome at TIP.

On Becoming an Independent Agency

I met with Louis Nine, explained the situation at TIP, and asked him to allow me to form an independent nonprofit. He agreed, and the Neighborhood Self-Help Older Adult Project Inc. was born. What follows are highlights:

1. The programs:
   a. The wellness program is a good example of how Maggie and I assumed separate but mutually reinforcing roles. I was for teaching the seniors to become activated patients.

      Maggie brilliantly developed a curriculum based on training materials she gathered from the medical literature. The aim was to inform older people how to deal with the chronic illnesses of diabetes, arthritis, and cancer. Featured were diets appropriate to each illness and exercises suited for older people.

      I wrote a proposal featuring that curriculum and ideas, and we succeeded in receiving a grant.

      Maggie then shared our curriculum with the nursing faculty advisor at the College of Mount Saint Vincent in the North Bronx, and she was happy to affiliate with us. Two nurse interns a semester for several semesters were assigned to N-SHOPP. Maggie taught them the curriculum, and they then taught it to the older adults.

      Among other exercises, I demonstrated to the interns how to teach race walking. The nurses learned the techniques easily. What was amusing was that many of the women had a cultural resistance to swinging their hips, which is essential to race walking. They were brought up to believe that "good girls" do not swing their hips. Sometimes the students called on me to demonstrate, and the women found it funny that a man was comfortable doing that. I reassured them that race walking was an Olympic sport. We received plaudits from the school, and the seniors loved working with the young future nurses.

b. Among several other grants I obtained as executive director and fund raiser, the largest was from the United Way. We trained many of the more capable older adults to provide other seniors information about services and resources that might meet their needs. Once trained by us and carrying resource notebooks, our members went into the waiting rooms of social security offices, medical and other facilities that older people use. They asked each person individually if they wanted information of other services available to them. During the frequently long waiting times our members were well received and succeeded in providing information to many of their own generation who often were unaware they were eligible for the help they badly needed.

c. For three summers we took our members to the Hudson Guild Farm (a beautiful five-hundred-square-mile campsite in New Jersey). It was owned and operated by the Hudson Guild, a settlement house located in the Chelsea area of Manhattan, and founded by John Elliot, a former leader of NYSEC. The Guild ran a senior citizen center whose members also spent summer weeks at the Farm. One day the farm director told me that the older people I brought were so much more appreciative of the program and facilities, and so much more willing to assist in cleaning up and being generally helpful, than the Hudson Guild seniors. He wanted to know why. I told him that senior citizen center programs are based on the concept that older people tend to need to be on the receiving end of service. I believe that leads to passivity. At N-SHOPP, on the other hand, we believe older people want to reassure themselves that they can not only do better than expected in taking care of themselves but that they can also do well serving each other.

2. The politicians:
When Louis Nine died, we no longer received funding from New York State, but our program had expanded, as had my role among senior citizen community center staff in a wide area surrounding our office on Southern Boulevard.

With his death there was no one in the New York State Legislature whom we knew well enough to request substitute funding. So I spoke to and received one thousand to five thousand dollar grants from several elected officials on city and state levels. Eventually they were convicted of one form of corruption or another. The one politician who secured more funds for us than all the others combined was Fernando Ferrer. Freddie, as he was affectionately called, had been a highly respected city council member when Stanley Simon, the Bronx Borough president, was convicted of receiving $50,000 in cash and free travel from the Wedtech factory officials in exchange for helping secure a governmental contract for the firm.

When the Democratic Party power brokers had to choose a new borough president, they needed someone who was "clean" or incorruptible, and they picked Freddie Ferrer. Their desperation was based on the fact that prominent politicians and elected officials, other than the ones who funded us, were convicted and served prison time. Notably among them were former Bronx Democratic Party boss Stanley Friedman and Congressmen Mario Biaggi and Robert Garcia. I found ways to impress Freddie Ferrer with our program long before Louis Nine died.

As a close political ally of Louis Nine, Councilman Freddie Ferrer would from time to time visit our programs. So when we needed funds to continue, he helped secure a large grant from the city, administered by the New York Department of Aging.

Upon becoming borough president, Freddie Ferrer contracted the Regional Plan Association to think through possible projects and policies for his new administration by bringing together heads of nonprofits, academic and community leaders.

I was asked to participate, and I joined the committee on drug abuse, which I was dealing with in my own neighborhood as chair of the Lower East Side Call for Justice. I chose this committee as I was utterly opposed to the "War on Drugs." I believed then, as I do now, that this policy has succeeded in incarcerating addicts who needed treatment, not long prison stays.

Despite intense resistance from committee participants, including the head of the Regional Plan Association, I was able to convince most of the attendees of that drug abuse committee to recommend holding a forum on the issue. I learned from one of the BP's assistants, however, that Freddie did not welcome my initiative, but I persisted. When I spoke to Freddie, he was adamant in opposing such a forum.

Although N-SHOPP's funding from the city was secure, when I needed a separate grant of a few thousand dollars in public funds as a requirement for securing a huge grant from the Robert Wood Johnson Foundation on cancer prevention, Freddie turned me down, knowing that we had earned a very good chance for the grant and what his refusal would mean.

I wondered if it was because I promoted the forum on drugs knowing that he would be opposed to it, thus causing him some embarrassment. After my retirement, and as chair of the Lower East Side Call for Justice, I recommended that we interview candidates for the 2001 election for mayor of New York City. The only candidate who met with us in person was B. P. Freddie Ferrer. The others sent representatives. It seemed that I was back in his good graces. A few months later, I was invited to attend the Gramercy/Stuyvesant Independent Democratic Club for interview sessions with the candidates for mayor. When Freddie Ferrer, one of the candidates, saw me, he announced emphatically that I was "a terrific person." I guess he was telling me that he forgave me for putting him in a politically untenable situation by defying him regarding illegal drugs, and now he needed my support.

My scorecard and balancing act in dealing with former elected officials who provided funds for N-SHOPP and then were convicted of corruption was as follows:

Bronx Borough President Stanley Simon combined his grant to us with the amount we received from Council Member Freddie Ferrer. As indicated Simon spent a few years in prison. So Ferrer, who worked closely with Simon for a time, was chosen to replace him because of his honest reputation, which he holds to this day.

State Senator Pedro Espada gave us $1,000 and then called all of his grantees to a meeting. Unknown to us, he also invited the regular Bronx political establishment who opposed his electoral ambitions. He acted as if we came to support him. I was furious, and years later, when he was sentenced to five years for stealing money from the Soundview Health Center that he ran, I was not sympathetic, to say the least.

State Assemblyman Efrain Gonzalez Jr. raised $5,000 for us and was subsequently convicted of stealing hundreds of thousands of dollars from nonprofit groups to cover personal expenses and was sentenced to seven years in prison. Of the five elected officials who raised money for N-SHOPP, two had good records, Assemblyman Nine and BP Ferrer, and three were convicted of misusing their office for personal economic gain. I am fully confident that all five supported our program because they wanted to be identified with N-SHOPP.

After I retired in 1993, I stayed on as a part-time fund raiser/consultant for a year and a half. Since then N-SHOPP grew tremendously, especially under the leadership of Evelyn Laureano, the present executive director. Evelyn has won contracts that have added several new services to the self-help program—case management, crime victim assistance, and a senior center. The program now reaches many more people in a more comprehensive way. If Maggie were alive, I am sure she would be as proud as I am. As two white social workers setting up shop in an inner-city neighborhood, we were fiercely tested. For example, we faced:

Resistance from power brokers in the Hunts Point community

Criticism from the professional social work community for accepting a "member item" from an elected official

Loss of almost all funding when Assemblyman Nine died

Meeting temporarily in a small room of a bank because a fire in our building severely damaging our office

Nevertheless, N-SHOPP now in its thirty-seventh year, has engaged many older adults who have enriched each other's lives.

PART VI
My First Hard Cover
Published Essay

One

THE COLOR OF HIDDEN BIAS

(Originally Delivered as a Platform Address at the New York Society for
Ethical Culture, April 3, 2011)
"Overcoming a Heritage of Prejudice"

Background:

S horter versions of this address were published by *Politic365*, an African-American online daily, and the *Dialogue*, a newsletter of the American Ethical Union. The editors, in turn, called the submissions astonishing and remarkable. Then, when it was published in a hard copy magazine, the March/April 2012 edition of *The Humanist*, I felt great, but as I became busy, I didn't think to see how it was doing on the Internet. A year later a friend called and said that my article was on sale at Amazon.com for $9.95.

I then Googled it and found that it was duplicated by sixteen online magazines (three offered it free for subscribing), placed on file in the Villanova University Library, used by Questia as a tutorial for students, listed as a reference in a scholarly article about police reform, posted for the entire Black History Month on The New York Society for Ethical Culture web page in February 2013, and it received 3,369 views as of April 2013 in *The Humanist* online magazine.

I knew, when I gave up my rights to *The Humanist*, that I was giving up control over its use by others. Nevertheless, when I found out that it entered cyberspace, I felt great but completely left out of the dialogue about the issues I raised.

I spoke again of the article at an AEU Lay Leadership Summer Camp in July 2012, and several participants, despite having a social justice value system, admitted to being aware of their hidden biases.

My most gratifying praise came from several people who said that what I wrote relieved them of a long-held sense of shame about a bias that was implanted before they were aware of its meaning. Having struggled unsuccessfully to rid themselves of it, they were most grateful upon learning how to control it.

http://thehumanist.com/magazine/march-april-2012/first-person/overcoming-hidden-biases#.V69GmRyTxB4.email

On the anniversary of Martin Luther King Jr.'s assassination on April 4, 1968, an unintended consequence of the Civil Rights movement still gets little attention. The movement so transformed the way we thought about the relationship between blacks and whites that many white Americans became ashamed to admit to having a bias toward their fellow citizens who were black.

In his 2010 book, *The Hidden Brain*, Shanker Vedantam indicates that we form biases in the early months and years of our life. He asserts that this process takes place independently of the parents' influence. He states that children's biases can develop no matter how hard a parent tries to shield his or her young ones from them.

I believe a major unfinished aspect of the Civil Rights movement is the need to face and overcome our own individual biases. We should realize that we need not be ashamed of biases formed years before we were able to keep them from our young, impressionable brains.

I personally have known that I've held a deep bias toward blacks for about sixty years. When I say this most people I know don't believe it because they're aware of my belief system and activism in promoting civil and human rights. They may also know that I married Charlotte, an African-American woman, in 1953. We shared our biases with each other and we both had confidence that we could move past them.

Until recently, however, I wondered why I couldn't get rid of my prejudice, which lies below the surface, until I see a black face as an anchor on TV. In a split second, I wonder why that face is black and not white. In another split second, I recognize that my initial perception is counter to my conscious belief system and I dismiss it as unwanted.

In a 2009 *New York Times* op-ed, Charles M. Blow referred to studies concluding that most whites have a hidden racial bias. Blacks were shown to have biases toward whites, though not as frequently. As Blow summarized it: "Researchers were able to ameliorate whites' racial bias by teaching them to distinguish black people's faces from one another. Basically, seeing black people as individuals diminished white people's discrimination. Imagine that."

After years of facing skepticism when I told people that my brain must be hardwired for a negative attitude, social scientists appeared to agree with me.

As a white man living in a black family for the last fifty-eight years, and having served people of color as a social worker in inner cities, I can attest to having prejudice toward blacks and learning how to act without it. The key, I think, is to fully acknowledge it. Malcolm Gladwell discusses this phenomenon in his 2005 book, *Blink: The Power of Thinking without Thinking*. He quotes a psychologist, Keith Payne, who writes that, "When we make a split-second decision, we are really vulnerable to being guided by our stereotypes and prejudices, even ones we may not necessarily endorse or believe." Gladwell goes on to write that when one of our own hidden biases flashes before us, "we need to wait a beat before identifying the object in an unbiased way…the giant computer in our unconscious needs a moment to do its work."

A look at how police confront racial bias is very informative. There is now a method of training, recently implemented by the New York Police Department that helps officers recognize and overcome bias. It uses research that indicates that when police officers believe their lives are in danger, they become so frightened that they are no longer able to recognize body language. When facing a person of color, officers too often think stereotypically and believe that the person is carrying a gun or a knife and is ready to use it.

In the training, the officers are taught to wait a split second before determining whether or not to shoot. With repeated virtual training an officer is able to put his or her bias aside, recognize the person's body language, and act appropriately. NYPD Commissioner Raymond Kelly recently announced a sharp decline in shootings by police officers. We can presume that the bias training was an important factor in that reduction.

After white people assure themselves that they aren't under the control of their bias, they may feel free to be as critical of individuals whose skin color differs from their own as they feel is warranted. This could lead to much more honest and even rewarding experiences.

So now you know my story. I do hope you find it worthwhile, and I hope the day will come when we can share our stories, not out of a sense of confession, but out of a sense of satisfaction and a sense of victory over our demons.

Abe Markman got his master's degree in social work from NYU. He was the founder and former executive director of the Neighborhood Self-Help Older Persons Project in the South Bronx, and in 2010 was the recipient of the Community Service Award of the New York Society for Ethical Culture.

PART VII
The Color of Tomorrow

Toward the Survival of the Human Species:
A Unified Field Theory of Survival

My faith is fueled by the wondrous evolution
And untold possibilities of humanity
Bravely facing the unknown.

A. M.

Introduction to this chapter:

To prevent steadily worsening living conditions for the next two or three generations and for our species to survive intact into the twenty-second century, the powers that be will have to begin to target their efforts toward economic justice and environmental sustainability. More and more people will have to see themselves as members of a human community searching for ethical ways to interact and solve problems.

My fervent hope is that we become one human family seeking answers to how the universe was born.

Ours is a planet that may be the most, or among the most, nurturing places for life to exist in all the heavens. Do we not have an obligation to preserve our precious home? Do we not have an obligation to preserve life, and especially intelligent human life, even before we have discovered how it arose? Do we not have an obligation to try to discover the enigma within an enigma of how the universe came into existence?

Humanity's Epitaph
They sailed past hades,
Climbed heaven's gate,
Took a giant lunar step,
Sighted the "God Particle,"
And the Big Bang's Inflation,
Heard gravity whine,
A star cluster wail,
But they were deaf to global thunder,
Hence, they died before they knew why they were here.

The poem is dedicated to those who are committed to changing the last two lines to read:

And they heard the global thunder,
Hence, they lived to learn
How and why they were here.

A. M.

A Unified Field Theory of Survivability

As humans we have the capacity to devote countless resources toward the survival of our species. Nevertheless, we are seeing rising exploitation and destruction of the eco-system on which we depend. As a result, intelligent life on this planet is seriously threatened.

The Unified Field Survivability Theory has four premises:

(1) We must move much more rapidly toward reliance on renewable, clean energy;

(2) Our world-wide economic system must be effectively regulated and managed, with the aim of achieving fairness and stability;

(3) Ethical humanism and progressive action must be vigorously and nonviolently pursued;

(4)   A species-wide mission to unravel the mystery of the origin of the universe should be undertaken, even if it takes generations of scientific and soul-searching effort, and I call it.

The Ultimate Quest, or UQuest.

It calls for nothing less than a planetwide reawakening and embrace of the wonder, awe, mystery, and majesty of the night sky. In the full paper, I intend to seek answers to questions that start with the miniscule and reach toward the ultimate:

Why do ants and other insects have an inherent ability to survive as a species while humans do not?

What do we humans have to learn about ourselves and overcome so that we can share our planet in peace and in survivability?

Can progressive change be considered ethical and successful if severe backlashes are not anticipated and avoided?

Why has the vast majority of our species deadened the wonderment needed to solve our most profound mystery: How or Why the universe came into existence?

Here are some of my present understandings, assumptions, and assertions.

Most likely, our earliest ancestors were curious, fearful, bewildered, and suspicious, experiencing a solar eclipse or seeing the night sky as a magical dome of myriad configurations of pulsating pips of light, streaking, showering, or at times crash-landing nearby, causing shock, death, and destruction.

It is the view of anthropologists that the first humans' sense of awe, wonder and mystery was suppressed by the great storytellers, shamans, and priests. The purpose was to ease fears of the unknown suspended far above anyone's reach.

They were told compelling stories that in millions of retellings took on biblical dimensions. They calmed the fears of much of humanity.

Some scientists and philosophers have called our need to believe in a supernatural being the GOD gene. I found this explanation in Wikipedia:

The God gene hypothesis proposes that human spirituality is influenced by heredity and that a specific gene, called vesicular monoamine transporter 2 (VMAT2), predisposes humans towards spiritual or mystic experiences.

I will try to show that the GOD gene is really a wonderment or mystery gene.

Why would such a reemergence into consciousness of the wonderment gene and the ultimate search be so very important? Because if a large majority of members of our species embrace it, there is a better chance that we would see ourselves as one people under the banner of a common mission.

Rabbi Naomi Lev in her book, *Einstein and the Rabbi*, quotes the famous mathematical genius with this excerpt from a condolence letter to a friend who saved the lives of thousands of children from the Holocaust but afterward confronted the death of his own son:

> A human being …experiences himself, his thought, and feelings, as himself separate from the rest … a kind of optical delusion of his consciousness. The striving to free oneself from that delusion of his consciousness is one issue of a true religion.

Rabbi Lev states that Einstein was referring to the connections humans have to each other and to the universe and to the need to foster a worldwide caring community.

Establishing such a community under the banner of a species-wide mission may seem worthy of the most far-fetched sci-fi novel. But who can deny that with each breakthrough scientific discovery, there is a chance that we will begin to realize that most people marvel at the same magic-like phenomena?

And with help from rabbis like Naomi Lev and many other interfaith and secular humanists, we can bring into consciousness our connections to each other, our need to care for each other, and our capacity to keep wondering.

In so doing, wouldn't we have a better chance to eventually overcome tribal, cultural, gender, ethnic, racial, and national differences long enough to survive to find out *how* and/or *why* we are here.

If South Africa and Columbia can reconcile profound conflicts within each of their countries, what is to stop the rest of us from reconciling our differences?

Does it have to require a continued series of wars based on ethnic cleansing as in Europe, Croatia, and Rwanda for us to put aside differences and begin to work across borders?

Can a nation denounce its own Aryan or racist belief systems without being virtually blown apart in bloody conflagrations?

Will owners of gas-, coal-, and methane-producing corporations and their financial allies need to lose two or three of their mansions, summer and winter homes, across seas and on mountainsides swallowed up by hurricanes, wildfires, and earthquakes before they accept the science of climate change?

Does humankind have to wait for calamities on grand scales to learn how to survive?

How close do we have to get to extinction before our self-imposed veil of ignorance is thrown aside?

My question is: wouldn't a science-based, specieswide mission help to mitigate the urge for racial dominance, ethnic cleansing, tribal conflict, and war?

Such a mission could contribute heavily to the establishment of a planet wide caring community striving to bring out the best in each of its members while embracing an increasingly compelling quest into the unknown. Although the answer to the quest, I firmly believe, will come through scientific discovery, it will require religious fervor for it to be successfully pursued.

Rationale for an "Ultimate Quest":

As human life has taken 13.7 billion years to emerge on planet Earth, we may be unique in the vastness of the universe. Whether or not intelligent life exists on distant planets, I believe it is incumbent upon us to find ways to survive as a species. It would be a tragedy if humanity were to disappear before we unraveled the greatest mystery of all: how and by what means the universe came into existence. Though I do not believe there is a supernatural, caring God, I wonder how a universe existing in the range of infinite complexity can emerge out of nothing.

Although I have a sense of reverence for Felix Adler, the founder of the Ethical Culture movement, for his profound and lasting contribution to humanism, ethical living, and social justice, I disagree with one of his assertions.

In *Life and Destiny*, a collection of Adler's early platform addresses, he is quoted as saying that "Of the origins of things we know nothing, and can know nothing."

On the other hand, John Dewey, whose views are considered more closely identified with the Ethical Culture movement in the modern era, asserted that scientific discovery may uncover the ultimate mystery of the universe. In his book *A Common Faith*, he writes:

> "[Faith] trusts that the natural interactions between man and his environment will breed more intelligence and generate more knowledge, provided the scientific methods that define intelligence in operation are pushed further into the mysteries of the world ..."

Although it might take a century or more to solve the UQuest, why not celebrate with the physicists and astrophysicists every brilliant and spectacular inch they bring forward? If mankind is thrilled by earthly challenges like climbing the highest mountains, what prevents us from joining the most challenging search of all: *What caused the BIG BANG to happen?*

Whether humans will ever succeed is beyond knowing at this time but isn't there a potential for vast numbers of people to eventually embrace the scientific process leading to an answer?

Though the physics and math are beyond the comprehension of most of us, there are those who exhibit phenomenal capacity to explain in layman's terms the underlying concepts of what is known, and what theories are being pursued. Carl Sagan's early PBS *COSMOS* series, Neil deGrasse Tyson's follow-up to Sagan's series on FOX, Morgan Freeman's Science Channel series *Looking through the Worm Hole*, Brian Greene's PBS series *Nova*, and Robert Lawrence Kuhn's PBS and CUNY series *Closer to Truth* are prime examples.

Although there is a growing movement away from traditional religion, that movement is essentially indifferent to such concepts as the "Ultimate

Quest." The atheists, agnostics, humanists, and Ethical Culturists whom I have encountered have strong feelings of liberation from "oppressive religious traditions" but most have not cohered around a mission of their own.

As many do not want to be identified with "creationism," they shy away from asking from whence the universe came. They are reluctant to ask whether or not there is a pulse of discovery in mathematical formulae or in nature.

THE UNIFIED FIELD SURVIVABILITY THEORY (UFST): MEASURING SUCCESS

The evidence is clear that the earth is warming at a highly dangerous rate; the oil, coal, and methane producers have closed their eyes to reality; and the global financial system is failing uncountable numbers of people.

Implementation of the elements of the UFST could prove to be mutually reinforcing. For example, discoveries in mathematics, quantum mechanics, and astrophysics may lead to green energy applications. Ethical humanism has the potential to lead to conflict resolution.

Achieving equality, justice, and the moderation of the steep rise and fall of markets is essential. This means the wealthiest financiers and corporate leaders who are the most powerful people globally — will need to change profoundly and become moral agents. This is one of humankind's greatest challenges.

The challenge can be met if the powers that be recognize early enough that in their own self-interest and in the interests of everyone, actions to alter our present path are of critical importance.

It can and must be met by the global public's willingness to take strong but ethical, non-violent action to protect the environment and promote social and economic justice for all.

Our progeny born in our lifetime will probably not in their lifetime be present when the greatest of all mysteries is solved. But if the unified field theory takes hold, their descendants may not only have an improved chance to survive themselves but their way of life might be constantly enhanced with an increased sense of brotherhood.

Why the Universe Exists

Based on hearing countless astrophysicists interviewed by Robert Lawrence Kuhn on the PBS series *Closer to Truth*, I have the following thoughts on why there is a universe.

Several scientists have conjectured that the universe appears to be designed for life to exist. Others have speculated that there is a mathematical equation to be found that one day will reveal the answer to the UQuest. Others like Raymond Kurzweil, an award winning, pioneering engineer in astrophysics, believes it may be possible someday to build a new and separate universe!!

If a new universe can be built, what prevents us from learning how our own universe arose? Such a planetwide or universewide search that today hardly registers on most people's mental and emotional radar screens, will hopefully become more and more compelling when a human sets foot on Mars or we discover signs of life in outer space. It may not happen until the day we are able to leave our solar system or communicate with an intelligent being far off in space. However long it takes to capture the imagination of our entire species, it may be our precious imagination that enables us to survive long enough to know the "unknowable."

Max Tegmark, associate professor of physics, science director, MIT, said on PBS's *Closer to Truth*, Saturday, September 17, 2016, that probably we will eventually understand whether the universe has a reason. He was interviewed by Robert Lawrence Kuhn, the host/physicist, who agreed by saying that we are learning so much at such a rapid rate that it is likely that we will uncover the mystery of all mysteries.

Based on this conjecture I am wondering whether the universe was, in fact, born to become a vastly expanding nest for the birth, nurturing, and evolution of intelligent life.

And — is it possible that human-type beings with equal or higher intelligence lived fourteen billion years ago in another universe, and is it possible they knew how to give birth to the Big Bang?

Because it took humanoids four and a half billion years to evolve on earth, is it preposterous to consider the possibility that other intelligent life evolved on another universe before the Big Bang?

Unless you have listened to these highly regarded scientists being interviewed on *Closer to Truth*, you may find the premises underlying the above questions incredible, but I think not if you Google: *Closer to Truth/Are We Living in a Simulation?*

Of course, the most enigmatic question of all is who or what started the starter, and started the starter of the starter of the starter —ad infinitum?

As an amateur philosopher, I cannot accept the view advanced by some scientists that the universe was incubated in and inflated from out of a vacuum. They insist that all vacuums have some residual matter and enough to inflate into a universe like ours. Assuming these scientists are right, where did the matter in the imperfect vacuum come from, and how was it ignited to produce trillions of star systems?

You might ask, with all the unsolved problems we face, why take on one that will probably not affect most people's lives today? But what if the UQuest eventually becomes global and helps save the human race?

Although slowing down global warming is the most pressing existential challenge we face, growing support for the UQuest may in the long run incentivize more people to become climate change activists worldwide.

More powerful and more dazzling than a Close Encounter or a Magical Meet-Up with an ET are quests that are likely to open the flood gates of understanding of the fate of our universe:

- How the spark of life on earth was ignited
- How the amazing, intricate, and complex ways plants grow and survive and interact with other species
- What the nature of dark energy and dark matter is
- How all fundamental subatomic forces are united into a single theoretical framework, or the physicists' unified field theory

Although the prospects might seem far-fetched, I believe humanoids one day will relish every discovery and will pass the torch of knowledge in the colors of multi-multi-intergenerational time. The joy of the quest by scientists will be shared by people of all backgrounds and passed on until the truth is discovered.

Just imagine a team of our distant offspring being hailed as the discoverers of the universal quest!

If not an earthling, maybe it will be a citizen of a species from another planet who will be present at the ultimate revelation. If we do find other intelligent beings in our universe I do hope we will have evolved enough to offer them acceptance, respect, endless awe and an invitation to join the Ultimate Quest.

In short, I believe that if we free ourselves to revel in the mystery of how the universe arose, we may become aware that we need each other to survive long enough to visit the ultimate conception. This could happen if we firmly establish the validity of the unified field of economic equality and stability, environmental sustainability, and — deep and abiding respect for one another—all under the banner of a shared yearning for the truth of how we got here and whether, indeed, there is a reason why we are here.

A Review of this Chapter

/"Abe Markman proposes a quest of discovery that has the power to unite humanity behind the one thing we all share, namely our origins. We all ultimately belong to the same human family, the same animal kingdom, the same evolutionary tree, the same planet, galaxy, and universe. We are each of us children of the Big Bang, whose wonder and mystery calls us to understand it, and in so doing, understand ourselves."

Chris Everett is a scientist and engineer working for NASA in the areas of system safety and risk management. He has degrees in physics, computer science, education, and reliability engineering."

SECTION 2
More about My Family of Birth

Mom and Pop, 1913

This section is devoted to sketches of my parents and a dream of brotherly forgiveness. If included in Section 1 they might have distracted the reader from the main theme of the book. However, placed here, they hopefully will give added perspective to that theme.

Also it includes brief reflections of the remarkable Leaders of the Ethical Culture movement that I have known, as well as acknowledgments.

Chapters One and Two

SKETCHES OF POP AND MOM

My Father
Isadore "Izzy" Markman
(1886–1974)
The Leader of His Clan

Sarah, my grandniece, thinks that my father bequeathed to us a writer's gene. I think it is a storytelling gene. There were other genes I think he passed along as well: love of family, entrepreneurship, and an ability to bring people together in a circle of fun or politics. Most important for me was that while in his late seventies, my father had the capacity to grow.

Writing about him brought me to a deeper, better-rounded understanding of Pop, and I will try to give you an idea of his character and a greater understanding of why he was the first of my closest kin to insist on Charlotte's acceptance into our family.

My writing might also give you an idea of how his philosophy, political beliefs, and social skills, or lack thereof, may have influenced me. His father, Mordichai, was an untrained rabbi (or rebbe) in Minsk, Russia. He wanted his son to become an ordained rabbi and enrolled my father in a theological training program when he was four years old. Pop told me that the study of Judaism required thinking through contending sides of philosophical dialogues. It was too much for a youngster to take in, and he refused to continue his religious studies.

As a teenager Pop became an apprentice jeweler and later brought those skills with him to America. Before leaving Russia, he witnessed the beginning of revolutionary times and was attracted to the Trotsky brand of socialism and atheism. Trotsky was an opponent of Stalin, as was my father. What many people learned about Stalin through the media, books, and documentaries I learned from my father as a child, (for example, the systematic starving of peasant farmers for their resistance to collectivization.)

I was with Pop the moment it was announced on the radio that Trotsky was assassinated in Mexico. With a burst of anger, he blamed Stalin. His attitude influenced my own negative feelings toward Stalin and his dictatorial rule.

Pop left Russia in 1907 to avoid being drafted into the Tsar's army. When he was settled here in the United States, he brought his brother, Abe, and sister, Gussie, to this country. Later he welcomed two nephews, Max and Alex, who came through Canada as undocumented immigrants. Max and Alex were both communists. I always thought that was why they entered the country illegally.

Sometime after arriving, my father started a costume jewelry business with his brother Abe and did very well. After a dispute between them, Uncle Abe started his own costume jewelry business with his son Manny, the father of Gary, who wrote the introduction to this book. Pop married my mother, Mary Goldberg, around 1911. As mentioned, they had five children, and I am the youngest and the only one surviving.

I was told by my brothers that before the Great Depression, my father had savings worth about $125,000, mostly invested in the stock market. That would be the equivalent of about two million dollars today. Pop also owned a movie theater in Brooklyn and a tenement house in the Bronx.

Unfortunately, with the stock market crash, he lost almost all of his stocks, the movie theater, and the tenement. My oldest brother, Milton, told me that I should have known him in the old days. Before the economic collapse, he was a vibrant spirit, but afterward and during most of my preteen years, he was in a blue mood, resulting mainly from the loss of almost all of his financial assets accumulated over three decades. Those assets were made through business acumen and strenuous labor. For example, he took turns with my brothers, standing for a few hours most working days ladling out a molten alloy at six hundred degrees Fahrenheit into bronze jewelry molds. His pockmarked arms were witness to the highly painful, red-hot droplets that bounced off the kiln. Though most of his rhinestone items were levels below high-priced costume jewelry, most people still could not afford to buy them during the Depression.

As bad as things were, when I was just old enough to choose what candy I wanted, he called me every night just before leaving work and asked what kind he should bring. Later in life it occurred to me that he had differences with my mother about me. He openly showed his love for me in the face of my mother's harsh treatment.

Pop was deeply grateful to FDR for the Home Loan Association, which subsidized the cost of our three-family house in the Bronx. Though we lived in a seven-room ground-floor apartment, we hardly had enough to pay our bills.

As mentioned, he would send me, a ten-year-old, to the grocer to ask if we could get food and pay later. I was also sent upstairs to collect the rents from the tenants. I do not remember ever collecting any.

As business gradually improved, my father started buying Buicks. As the only one in the large extended family to have a car, he would pick up relatives and bring them to our house and tell us stories. He loved to read his favorite articles from the *Forvitz* (*The Daily Forward*). He delighted in the cries for H—E—L--P from newly arrived immigrants seeking advice or, in contrast, from movie stars who changed their names to avoid being the targets of anti-Semitism.

The house often resounded well into the night with politics from many points of view. Though I was too young to add my voice, I listened attentively.

I loved it when our communist cousins, Max and Alex and Alex's wife, Yolanda (I can't recall her real name), visited. Yolanda was a journalist working for the *Freiheit* (*Freedom*) a Yiddish daily of the Communist Party. She told of her political assignments overseas. Huddled into our living room, the family had animated but quite civil discussions along with my non-communist but left-of-center brother, Sidney, my conservative-leaning brother, Milton, and my father, the Trotskyite. When put to bed early, I would strain to listen until I fell asleep. My love for politics and circles of friendly dialogue was implanted in my soul on those nights.

Other instances of his storytelling were the times I had him all to myself. In the early 1930s, he would take me on walks in the Bronx. During those walks, we would talk, and he would explain all he knew about the beautiful but utterly clear starry skies and what people imagine they see in the constellations.

I was amazed when he explained that light takes only eight and a half minutes to reach the earth from the sun, even though it is nearly ninety-three million miles away. The chapter on "The Color of Tomorrow" was clearly influenced by these walks with the sky alive with unfathomable images that we observed with our naked eyes.

Much later, in the years of his fury at my marrying Charlotte, I was so angry with him that I was in denial of his abiding love. It was the character of that love and his fear of losing it that brought him to accept the marriage while almost every other member of the very large clan could not.

As far as bequeathing his storytelling to us, my son, Michael, had a book of children stories published in 1997 called *The Path*. In 2015, his educational comic book on Hurricane Sandy, *Surviving the Storm*, was completed. It was distributed widely, especially to school children and their parents. It is an often funny history of how three generations of our family continued to learn and share how to face a storm with some success. We were all thrilled to learn that he was been nominated this year, 2017, for an Emmy for a New Jersey TV program featuring him teaching art to children.

My daughter, Chandy, was a journalist/activist for African American Brooklyn weeklies. All through her teens and young adulthood, she kept journals, and three of her poems as mentioned were published in a book called *The Gap Tooth Girls: An Anthology*.

My grandniece Sarah is a professional editor of public school texts, and my grandson, Tariq, writes stories. Tariq, like his father, is a rapper. Michael was an exceptional rapper and performed with a wonderful band at a night club to loud applause, but he did not want to pursue it as he thought it would interfere with being a good husband and father and with his career in art.

Tariq wants to see how far he can go as a rapper. Also, in October 2016, he wrote the text for Michael's latest educational comic book with sensitivity and imagination and he gave me some good advice about the readability of a sketch in this book. As noted, I have recently had some success publishing articles.

Another example of Pop's fierce attachment to the family happened while I was attending college. It was shortly after the Second World War, when young couples had a hard time affording separate apartments. As a consequence, my sisters and their husbands and children all lived with my parents and me in a five-room apartment. I told my father that ten people living in one apartment caused us to run into each other's space constantly, and it was not working. My father said angrily, "We have *poifeck* harmony here!" and that ended the discussion.

Regarding my father's entrepreneurship, it may have had historical roots. On a question from Tiana, my granddaughter, I looked up the derivation of our last name, Markman. Its meaning is *market trader*. Furthermore, my father reported that he had an older close relative who owned a very large and successful factory in Russia. When the Bolsheviks came to power, they took control of his business and killed him.

Working in Pop's shop became a must for almost every male and some females in the family. In addition, he would bring work home, and my sisters and brothers and I would sit around the kitchen table and paste rhinestones into costume jewelry. At the age of eight or nine, I was assigned to apply the paste. My sister Esther was the fastest stone-setter. Her dexterity amazed me.

Milton and Sidney, my older brothers, after working full-time for my father for many years, continued the shop years after his death. Sidney's specialty was designing the jewelry, and Milton's was sales and promotion. Although they had widely different personalities, they worked well together.

I believe that my cofounding and running a social service agency in the last twenty years of my professional career was my way of emulating my father's business predisposition. Its acronym was Neighborhood SHOPP, named after the family's "shop." As mentioned above it was short for Neighborhood Self-Help Older Persons Project, Inc.

In regard to my father's seemingly innate ability to bring friends and family together in a circle, it must have rubbed off on me as it became an essential part of my social group work practice. The settlement movement was founded by Jane Adams, who introduced the circle as a means of bringing people together to discuss and improve conditions in their neighborhood. I have used the circle often during a sixty-two-year career of paid and volunteer work in inner-city neighborhoods with youth and older adults, in settlement houses, community centers, the N-SHOPP, and in my activism.

Also, in my ninety-second year, I am enjoying facilitating Ethics in the News, a monthly group discussion in the round at the Ethical Culture Society.

Another example of the impact of his entrepreneurship upon our family is that Pop's grandchildren have done well in commercial or commercially related careers, including accounting, insurance, large store managing, computer consulting, private social work practice, and art entrepreneurship.

So, what do you think? Was Pop bringing a business gene with him when he came to this country? Some of my father's grandchildren also had careers working with people as excellent teachers. Each one of Pop's qualities reinforced the others, and his love for family strongly influenced the success of his business. Even though he and my Uncle Abe had a serious conflict resulting in two businesses with two methods of manufacturing costume jewelry, they renewed their friendship and supported each other's businesses. (My Uncle Abe's method of casting jewelry was with plastic instead of bronze molds.)

Pop's enjoyment in telling stories and bringing people together were traits he used in the promotion of his business. He also used these skills to enhance the bonds between many members of our large, extended family.

So, was Sarah right about Pop's genealogical influence on our storytelling and was I right about his other influences on us? Was it serendipity or were his gene's really stirring things up in us?

My father, like all people, was far from perfect. He failed to acknowledge that my mother needed help bringing up five children and, later, caring for her grandchildren and many cousins. In addition, my father gave her no help cleaning and managing our large house on Ward Avenue or, later, our crowded five-room apartment on Townsend Avenue.

He hurt my mother in another way. He flirted with her sister, Ida, openly during family gatherings. As a consequence, my mother and Aunt Ida projected their intensified sibling rivalry upon their sons, Walter and me. Without realizing the source, at that time, our friendship became intensely competitive.

I found that I inherited some of his negative tendencies and have tried hard to overcome them. As a matter of fact, I sometimes acted the same way to Charlotte by praising a female associate at my job. It was Chandy who let me know that I was making Charlotte angry. I had not been aware of the impact I was having. When confronted by my daughter, I never spoke to Charlotte of my associate again.

My father also bequeathed to me his difficulty in setting limits. Believe it or not, it has only been recently that I have made progress in knowing when to cut down on my activism and start to take better care of myself.

In essence, without the genius to excel, except in his devotion to his family, Pop possessed the spirit of a renaissance man. Besides what I have already written about him, add this: he was constantly trying something new. Once, he attempted to invent a device to see inside eggs to check their health. In his late seventies, he began painting, despite ridicule from my siblings. He played tunes of well-known songs on the piano with one finger without ever having been trained and could add very large numbers in his head.

He seemed determined to enjoy his life and bring joy to his family. That is what he bequeathed to all of us, and in good measure, he succeeded.

Two

My Mother

Mary Goldberg Markman
(1890 — 1969)

I met my mother when I was eighty-six years old!

Until then I thought I knew my mother, but in truth, I knew her only in a very narrow sense. As I indicated earlier, I had determined that her harsh treatment was why I was so angry at her and at anyone who mistreated me or mistreated anyone else. In writing about her, however, I have come to a more rounded understanding of who my mother was. I have a feeling mixed with strangeness, revelation, warmth, and love.

As mentioned, the breakthrough occurred when Gary Markman, my recently discovered and treasured younger cousin, while editing an early draft of this book, read that my parents moved away from my two sisters and their families on Townsend Avenue to a smaller apartment a couple of miles away. Till he read about that, Gary was not aware that my mother and father invited Charlotte and me to dinner two or three times. According to the negative image I had portrayed of my mother, he wondered why I had not told him this. Below is what Gary read in an earlier draft:

> Because my mother rarely showed her love for me, I thought of ways to win her approval. So when I was about nine, I would find ways to

help her by washing windows, taking out heavy barrels of ashes from our coal-burning furnace, and rolling them up the fairly steep alley-way adjoining our house for the garbage men to take away. One time I decided to buy my mother some ice cream. I was so anxious to bring it to her that I ran with it, tripped, and it spilled over the sidewalk. I felt awful.

Much more significantly, what I wish I would have done differently happened when my mother asked if I would help her learn to read and write. When she had trouble, I was impatient with her, and she never tried again. I probably was retaliating. Nevertheless, I lost a great opportunity that could have changed her life and her attitude toward me.

At the same time, my two older brothers, who were thirteen and twelve years older than me, often said critical things about or to me. I loved my brother Milton. I looked up to him, but he would often say to the rest of the family when I was three or four years old, "You have as much sense as Abie the baby." My brother Sidney acted as if he didn't like me, and I had trouble liking him. He would complain that I was taking too long to do my homework, and later to finish college, even though he himself dropped out and didn't finish. Recently I was surprised but happy to learn from his daughter, my niece Barbara, that he was a warm and good father.

It was very hard for my mother, taking care of all of us, cooking, and cleaning our large house and, later, our overpopulated apartment. At the time I thought that was what every married woman with children did. I didn't know of any mothers who worked for salary outside the home.

My mother seemed always to be complaining. She wanted my two sisters to help with cleaning chores but would not explain what she wanted them to do. My parents' relationship could be encapsulated in a nightly ritual. Before my father came home from work, Mom would put white doilies on the arms of his favorite chair. As soon he sat down, too tired to wash up after casting costume jewelry for hours, my mother would attack with, "Look, Izzy, you're spoiling the doilies!"

Mom was always dissatisfied with what I was doing, how I was dressed when company came, and why I wasn't as good a student in school as Sidney had been. Right up to the time I left home, my mother was critical of me.

When she learned that I intended to marry Charlotte, my mother threatened to die of a heart attack. She told me that my brother Sidney thought I should be seen at the psychiatric ward at Bellevue Hospital. I called him and told him, "Keep the hell out of my life."

Returning to the time when my parents invited Charlotte and me to visit, she was as relaxed as I have ever seen her.

After Gary asked his question, I realized how I must have angered Mom and Pop by moving to Seattle and especially without sitting down with them and explaining why I was taking a job there. Probably due to their misunderstanding and their prejudice, they blamed Charlotte for taking me away from them.

Gary's question also reminded me that Milton once told me about my father's indifference to Mom's burdens and how he at times infuriated her.

What is more, I brought into consciousness pleasant memories of her that I had suppressed. I remembered how Mom was so embracing of her grandchildren till they reached about the age of four. What if the truth was that she loved us all to death until she thought we should be old enough to clean up after ourselves? What if I was one of those on the receiving end of a second loving, embracing parent at a time I was too young to remember!

I do definitely recall moments when my mother was fun to be with. One time when I was with her in the basement, and while cutting open a chicken, she found an egg. She cracked the egg open and said I could swallow its contents.

I then remembered how attentive my mother was to the black man who came on the coal delivery truck. One time he joined us in the basement and told us of his hard life in the South. The positive feeling he generated in me toward the plight of blacks was countered at other times by my mother's demeaning references to African Americans.

For several summers my parents rented a bungalow in Rockaway Beach in Brooklyn, New York. Once, when I was about fifteen years old, my mother and father were sitting on the porch. As I passed by, my mother said to my father, "We brought up Abie to be a prince." It was so out of character that I didn't know what to say.

Years later as a twenty-one year old college student, I joined my mother and father in the Catskills at a cousin's farm and mini-resort. I had recently written a pamphlet about my newly formulated naturalistic religion. It was a raw draft of the UQuest outlined above. Throughout my childhood my mother would tell me how God was going to punish me when I did something she didn't like. At the farm I noticed how relaxed my mother was, and I asked her, "Momma, isn't it true that nobody really knows whether or not there is a God?"

She answered, "Abie, it is true; nobody knows."

My mother's experience validates one of the main positions of the women's movement. Feeling besieged as a housewife with endless cleaning and cooking for nearly all of her life made her angry and bitter. Not knowing how to change her condition, she projected her anger at her two youngest children, my sister Marsha and me. She had inflicted so much pain that I buried memories of Mom that were bathed in her warmth and acceptance.

One of Mom's most consistently expressed attitudes was class consciousness. She identified with in-laws from upper-middle-class families. As a consequence she made me miserable because I didn't act like they were special. I came home late when they were invited to dinner, wearing a dirty shirt.

Mom was obsessively clean and always on time for special occasions. Because of her influence, I would feel compelled to be exactly on time, every time. I had to stop and remind myself that my mother was no longer hovering over me, and I could meet my obligations based on the circumstances of each situation.

As indicated, there is indirect evidence that she was nurturing to me till the age of memory or about three and a half or four. From then on her constant criticism dealt an enduring blow to my self-confidence. Although she invited Charlotte and me to their smaller apartment, her prejudice against blacks remained throughout her life, and when I was a child, it probably reinforced my own prejudice. Ironically, her treatment of me motivated me to overcome my shortcomings, and with tremendous effort, I was able to achieve some of my goals.

Nevertheless, there is a good possibility that if born in the age of women's' liberation, my mother would have had a happier life in which her suppressed warmth would have become a prominent characteristic.

In short, my mother bequeathed to me periods of warmth masked by tons of anger that led to my rejection of her conservative and religious beliefs. However, my father bequeathed to me the love of people, an inquiring mind, and a progressive philosophy.

It was their combined influence that fueled in me the determination to try to move justice an inch or so forward.

Three

THE COLOR OF FORGIVENESS

As I indicated earlier, my brother Sidney, twelve years my elder, did not treat me like his little brother but as a rival. That is why, sixty-nine years after we lived together in the same house, I was so pleased to have this dream:

> *I was with a group of people in our house on Ward Avenue when Sidney came by and asked me to follow him and said that he wanted me to pitch for his softball team.*
>
> *I told him that despite my advanced age, I knew how to pitch. I could even throw a curve ball.*
>
> *I followed him into a room where he left me with two very friendly, black, wiry-looking, and very intelligent dogs. You could see how much they wanted to talk and tell me how much they cared about me and then I woke up.*

Interpretation: Sidney was accepting me on his level...as a ball player. This may be my yearning for his acceptance. The dogs, I think, represented two meanings: (1) Sidney was giving Pal back to me, the dog that the family gave me and then gave away without involving me in the decision; and (2) his leaving me with the dogs was an acknowledgment that I was now capable of taking care of dogs; The fact that the dogs were very intelligent and responsive was a confirmation that Pal was not smart when he walked off and hung out with other dogs. Therefore, I should not have been held responsible for Pal's behavior, and he should not have been given away.

Also, Sidney's having black dogs was symbolic of his accepting my marriage. Finally, that there were two dogs getting along was my wish that Sidney and I could have had a warm relationship.

Although this was my dream and was my way of forgiving him, the dream reminded me that he did begin to change in reality.

For example, he wanted me to know years after my marriage that he had sponsored and taken into his home a Latino boy as a participant in the *New York Times* Fresh Air Fund.

Four

THE COLOR OF APPRECIATION

I want to thank the Leaders* of the American Ethical Union, the umbrella of the national ethical culture movement, for putting up with me for the last sixteen years. Here is my descriptive phrase for each Leader whom I have gotten to know. They all were and are charismatic and brilliant in diverse manifestations. In addition, I chose the quality that I admired the most about each one: Khoren Arisian keen political awareness; Anne Klaeysen — eloquent conveyer of the ethical/humanist religion; Kate Lovelady insightful; Hugh Taft-Morales inspirational; Curt Collier — ingeniously resourceful; Joe Chuman — outstanding scholar/philosophical historian/activist; Bart Worden — highly respected executive; Jone Johnson Lewis and Richard Kiniry — unmatched explainers of what is ethical.

*Our Leaders were trained in non-traditional, non-deistic, religious seminaries.

233

Last Words

With the help of the farmer's market, online shopping, meditation, exercise, reading, NPR radio and PBS television, pills, doctors, a loving family, friends, community, I'll keep writing in *The Color of Time and at the Edges of Change.*

Acknowledgments

I want to thank you for reading through to this point. I wore out several wonderful editors, trying with all they knew to improve my chances that you would come this far. Jim Bauer, an early member of the LES Call for Justice and the editor in the 1990s of a foreign affairs journal, volunteered and endured many revisions of essays on education and work/family issues. Those early efforts received one favorable reply from a magazine editor but were never published. But Jim—you tried and tried, and I am grateful to you. wherever you are. Nina Klippel, a wonderful and wise friend and former editor, tended to point me toward expressing what I really wanted to say with more clarity and fewer words. Also, she allowed me to use this sentence of hers verbatim: *"How do the amazing intricate and complex ways plants grow and survive and interact with other species?"* Alex Vitale, associate professor of sociology at Brooklyn College who became my co-chair of the Call for Justice in the late 1990s, read everything I wrote during those days. His conclusion was that it would be my personal story that would be considered, and sure enough, that is what happened. It was Pat Berens of Ethical Culture, as mentioned above, who helped me fulfill Alex's prediction with "In Person: Overcoming Hidden Biases," published in *The Humanist* magazine. Pat told me she would not give up no matter how many revisions I sent her.

My "at last" discovered cousin, Gary Markman, who wrote the introduction to this book, a published writer himself, was so very encouraging and helped endlessly with the editing.

The person who figured out what was wrong with my style was and is my dearest friend and partner, Virginia Arnold. She pointed out how I wrote while assuming the reader would fill in what I left out. My grandniece Sarah went through most of my writing and found many, many replications and non-explanations, along with her wise edits.

I asked my grandson, Tariq, to read one sketch, and he skillfully let me know when I was reader friendly and when I wasn't.

Andra Miller, the former president of NYSEC, has always been a wonderful supporter and edited the chapter on my advocacy projects at our wonderful building at the corner of Central Park West and Sixty-Fourth Street. It is the place we call "Ethical." Jason Marchi a publisher himself took a hard look and offered invaluable help despite having a highly busy agenda of his own.

To Fatima "Sudie" Stewart and all who kept me sane by restoring my apartment to livability twice a week — thank you, thank you!

What meant so much to me was when my son read and re-read drafts, made compelling suggestions, designed the front and back covers, told me that this book would be treasured by my grandchildren and all who lived after us in our family and especially how much better he understood me --- he said all this while going easy on my fumbling writing style.

And finally to the editor of CreativeSpace, the publisher, thanks for bringing me across the finish line with my sanity fighting its way back toward a degree of normalcy and my spirits in a pleasant state of recovery.

So please accept my profound appreciation to everyone mentioned who thought I had something to say — something that I hope was worth your time as well.

THE END

Made in the USA
Columbia, SC
21 August 2018